Taking care o[illegible]

All you need to k[illegible] oming, nutrition, and common disorders of Sphynx Cats

A guidebook for Sphynx owners

Expertengruppe Verlag

Taking care of a Sphynx Cat

All you need to know about general cat caring, grooming, nutrition, and common disorders of Sphynx Cats

A guidebook for Sphynx owners

Expertengruppe Verlag

Contents

About the author 6

Preface 8

What you need to know about your Sphynx 11

Fundamentals of feeding 19

Basic rules for feeding 20

If your Sphynx could decide for itself 27

What is on the menu? 30

Processed food 32

BARF 38

Home-cooked food 43

Vegetarianism and veganism 47

What you have to be particularly careful of when feeding your Sphynx 50

The water intake of your cat 52

The water requirement of your Sphynx 53

How to motivate your Sphynx to drink 57

The basics of grooming 62

Eye care 66

Skin and coat care 70

Ear care 77

Tooth care 81

Paw care 85

What you need to pay particular attention to when grooming your Sphynx. 91

Common disorders 94

Infestation of parasites 96

Mites 98

Ticks 102

Fleas 109

Gastro-intestinal disorders...115

Diarrhoea 116

Worms.. 121

Poisons and other problematic substances. 125

Cancers 129

Fever..132

Vaccinations 135

Panleukopenia und cat flu...139

Castration 143

Diseases typical for your breed 149

Checklist: For a healthy cat life 151

Checklist: Cat first aid kit...153

Special Chapter: Home-cooked cat food 154

Recipe 1: Salmon biscuits 155
Recipe 2: Wild potato biscuits 156
Recipe 3: Lung with rice 157
Recipe 4: Chicken with millet and egg 158
Recipe 5: Rice and ground beef cake 159
Recipe 6: Beef mix 160
Recipe 7: Wild turkey (BARF) 161
Recipe 8: Italian turkey 162
Recipe 9: Cat ice cream with banana and apple 163
Recipe 10: Cat ice cream with liver sausage and oat flakes 164
Conclusion 165
Space for your notes 167
Book recommendation for you 169
Did you enjoy my book? 175
References 177
Imprint 180

About the Author

Susanne Herzog is a true animal lover – to be more precise she is a cat lover, not surprisingly because she grew up in a household full of cats.

From an early age she developed her love of animals by helping out regularly in an animal shelter. For the first time she became aware of the darker side of keeping animals – with neglected, traumatised and practically unsocialised animals. This aroused her interest and she began to analyse how these things could happen. But even more important than investigating the reasons was for her to find out how most problems could be avoided in the first place. Building on this, she developed methods of how she could help animals with acute problem behavior to live a better and more normal life.

Susanne Herzog is not content just to help cats in the shelter, in which she still works on a voluntary basis, she also gives seminars for stressed cat owners several times a year. The experiences gained in her work and the feedback she has received from participants of her courses, gave her the idea of expanding the accessibility of her wide-ranging knowledge to a larger group of people in the form of a book.

Her aim is to help cat owners to set the right course between human and cat, from the very beginning, so that they can live happy and enriched lives together. She wants to avoid people from making mistakes right from the start which could cause bigger problems, leading to the cat being taken to a shelter.

After a long process of research, writing and correction, this guidebook emerged. In addition to general instructions for cat care, the needs of Sphynx cats are particularly addressed here. It is intended to provide every Sphynx owner with a guide to caring for their cat adequately and appropriately without any special prior knowledge. Every cat is worth receiving the necessary care that many uninformed cat owners are unable to provide.

Those of you who follow the tips in this guidebook can be sure to have many years of pleasure together with your exceptional companion.

PREFACE

Congratulations! You have chosen to share your life with a Sphynx, or you are about to make that choice. You will have a lot of fun with your new four-legged friend, a wonderful and incomparable breed, and soon you will not be able to imagine life without it.

It is scientifically proven, that having a cat as a pet can have a positive effect on us humans. You know it yourself, when you automatically begin to smile and be happy when your Sphynx greets you happily in the morning or after work. You know it, when you relax when your cat lies contentedly growling on your stomach while you watch a movie.

Cats are real stress-killers for us humans. Their quiet and even-tempered nature makes us feel better and happier. Even chronically sick people confirm that their cat makes them feel better. Your four-legged friend is a real bonus for your health.

For this reason, it is important that you take care of the health of your Sphynx as well. It is well known that if the cat is healthy, the human is happy too. Moreover, it is particularly important for you to keep an eye on your cat's health because often the cat itself cannot do that. Unfortunately, many cat breeds are overbred, which is the cause of many disorders and problems which could result in the owner being overburdened. I urge you at this point once again: Keep your eyes open when buying your cat!

Have a good look at the parents, if you can, and ask the breeder about disorders in the litters up to now. If a kitten is already disadvantaged at the time of purchase, you will probably have a lot of illness problems with it down the line. If you want to avoid that you should take care when buying your kitten and, if necessary, ask a vet for advice. Unfortunately, if you are buying from a shelter, it is unlikely that you will be able to get any information about the animals there, but on the plus side, shelter cats are usually examined by experienced vets.

Apart from breeding problems, modern processes and developments present challenges to our cats which their ancestors did not have in this form. Therefore, it is often necessary to take preventative steps which would make an unknowledgeable person shake his head and give you the typical argument that "tigers do not need that". If someone says that to you, I can only suggest ignoring it. After all, it is about the welfare of your cat.

In this guidebook, I want to give you the knowledge and self-confidence you need to be aware of your Sphynx's health and how to react if something is wrong.

It probably affected you as it affected me in the past: I suffered just as much as my cat and wanted to do everything possible to take away its pain, but I just did not know what to do.

Of course, it is not completely unavoidable that your cat may get sick – even with this guidebook. What you can do is to prevent some of the problems, even before they happen or at least to recognise them at an early stage.

Finally, it is important for me to stress that you will only receive tips and recommendations from me which I have gained through personal experience and which are generally accepted procedures in keeping cats. This guidebook cannot replace the visit to your vet. It is purely meant to give you the knowledge you need to assess the situation and to suggest some recommended procedures. If your Sphynx should suffer from acute or chronic problems, please contact your veterinary surgeon as soon as possible!

I wish you and your Sphynx all the best for the future and, above all, good health!

- Chapter 1 -

WHAT YOU NEED TO KNOW ABOUT YOUR SPHYNX

Did you know that, according to the International Federation of Cat Registries (FIFe), there are more than 48 official breeds of house cat? Your Sphynx is therefore only one breed among many. Of course, the various breeds have many things in common. After all, every cat originates in some form from its ancient ancestor, the predatory cat. You can see that with some breeds more than others.

I want to use this chapter to let you know exactly what you have let yourself in for with your Sphynx. The following is a short summary about this fascinating breed.

The Sphynx is unique – immediately striking and memorable. And there is a good reason for that: the fluffy fur is missing on this animal, which distinguishes it from other breeds. Instead of fur, it has a light fuzz on its body, which makes it a perfect cat for allergy sufferers. However, this is not the only reason why the Sphynx enjoys growing popularity. The demand for this unique breed is growing world-wide as it is not only striking because of its outward appearance, it also has a noble character.

Unfortunately, the popularity of this breed has its dark side too, and this is due to its lack of hair. This occurred because of an accidental mutation in a normal house cat which, unlike its parents, was born without hair. Its appearance caused a storm of enthusiasm resulting in the targeted breeding of hairless cats in 1966. Five years later, it was officially recognised, beginning its unstoppable race to popularity. Breeders all over the world were falling over themselves to get hold of this new breed and sensed large profits. Unfortunately, what began as a sign of beauty became an ordeal for many cats. The gene defect which causes the hairlessness can also lead to many cats being born without whiskers. This is an extremely important sensory organ for cats and those who are born without whiskers unfortunately have to suffer a very restricted lifestyle.

For this reason, there are very strict regulations about the breeding of these animals in Germany (and thankfully some other countries too), in an attempt to avoid the so-called "torture breeding"[1]. One of these rules, for example, states that the Sphynx breed must have whiskers, otherwise the

[1] Torture breeding is when vertebrates are intentionally bred to have inherited defects or diseases that cause distress and suffering

cats will come under the "torture breeding" rules and they will be forbidden in Germany. Breeders who break these rules will be committing an offence or even a crime, depending on the extent of the misdemeanour.

This breed has as many critics as lovers. This is not only due to the torture breeding, but also that they suffer from in-breeding. The gene pool is relatively small compared to other breeds and this can lead to problems with their general health. Responsible breeders, and there are many of them in Germany, know how to deal with both problems and if you are careful about your choice of breeder, there should be no repercussions for you.

This breed has really earned its popularity. It is very sociable, friendly and affable in every way, belying their strange appearance. At 3.5 – 6 kg, the Sphynx is a medium-sized cat. Its velvety soft skin does not have to be one colour. Patches and patters are allowed in various forms. This also applies to the eye colour, which is a great advantage because almost every Sphynx cat looks different. Contrary to other breeds, folds are encouraged, particularly between the ears and on the neck. The large, pointed ears are particularly striking, as are the large, lemon-shaped eyes. It can appear to look grumpy, which, however, is completely uncharacteristic for this breed.

Another impressive feature of this breed is its affectionate character and love of humans. It often chooses a human and becomes fixated with that person. Contrary to other breeds, the Sphynx shows its aversion to being alone quite openly and follows its owner's every step. It even likes going out for walks on the lead and loves the fetching games that we usually associate with dogs. If given the right training, your cat will have a lot of fun with that.

In addition to all that, Sphynx cats are very intelligent and attentive, always watching what is happening in its direct environment. Because of its playfulness and its enormous skill with its paws, these clever animals learn some things much quicker than its owners would like. For example, it is not unusual for a Sphynx to open doors by itself or turn water taps on and off, even though it has never been taught to do that.

These cats are not only good with children and other animals, they show great interest in them and are willing to play with them. They hardly ever show any aggressive behaviour, so they make very good pets for families with small children.

As far as their keep is concerned, Sphynx cats are satisfied with very little. They can be kept easily as house cats. Having said that, they love a garden and to watch nature and they are not averse to the occasional hunting adventure, but they do not need to be outside cats. It is more important for your Sphynx to have a close and loving relationship with you and the other members in your household. It needs to take part in family life and be integrated in family activities, irrespective of whether that takes place inside or outside the home.

Because of its lack of fur, it is not very weather-resistant and can easily get sunburned or cold during the winter. Using a sun cream which is suitable for cats in the summer or a warming lamp in the winter is never a bad idea. Do not be surprised if your Sphynx has a big appetite. The missing fur means that it uses more energy than other cats to keep its body warm. You should take care not to feed it too much as they have a tendency towards becoming overweight.

Now you know what a wonderful breed you have chosen! On the following pages, you will find additional information, in the form of a breed portrait, which sets out the current standards of the FIFe.

I will not be able to give you all the information about this wonderful breed in these few pages, but I hope I can give you a picture of what makes up your Sphynx. Naturally, there will be individuals which do not completely fit in with the profile, having stronger or weaker characteristics than those mentioned. However, I am sure you will be able to recognise your Sphynx in this description.[2]

[2] If you want to know more about raising or training your Maine Coon, I recommend reading the first two books of this series. You will find more information about those books at the end of this guidebook.

Photo	
Origin	Canada
Size	Medium Shoulder height: up to 40 cm
Weight	Females: 3.5 – 4.5 kg Males: 4 – 6 kg
Build	The body is slender and graceful. The legs are slim and medium-length, the hind legs are slightly longer than the front legs.
Head shape	The head is angular and pointed and the chin is strongly pronounced. The ears are large and pointed.
Eyes	The eyes are lemon-shaped and slanting. All colours are permitted.
Fur and colouring	This breed is hairless, having only a light fuzz on its body. The skin is velvety and folds are encouraged (particularly between the ears and on the neck).
Coat care	There is no need for coat care. However, the skin needs to be

	taken care of, particularly in the summer when it may be necessary to apply sun cream while the Sphynx is outside.
Character	This breed is particularly affectionate, friendly and loving. It is also self-confident and very intelligent.
Special characteristics	Because of its lack of hair, the Sphynx loses body temperature quickly, which it needs to offset by eating more than other breeds.

- Chapter 2 -

FUNDAMENTALS OF FEEDING

In this chapter you will discover what is important to bear in mind when feeding your cat. I will explain some rules about feeding and then describe the different types of food available in more detail, such as processed food, BARF, home-cooked food, vegetarian and vegan nutrition. After that, I will tell you about what you need to pay particular attention to, in the feeding of your Sphynx.

Finally, we will touch on a subject which is wildly underestimated by many: The water intake of your Sphynx. Much too often, owners fail to give their cats enough to drink. I will give you some tips on how to stimulate your cat to drink more.

Basic rules for feeding

It may sound surprising, but it is not so important what you feed your cat, but how. For this reason, I will tell you about how to feed your Sphynx in this chapter. There are many details that most cat owners do not know which could automatically damage their cat's health, or make feeding more difficult.

Once again, it is important for me to stress that these tips are derived from my own training, experience, extended research and many conversations with other cat trainers. If you are worried about anything, please check with your own vet before you start putting what you have read into practice.

One of the most common questions which cat owners ask me, and which is intensively discussed generally, is the question of how often a Sphynx should be fed. My initial answer is always: It depends!

Depends on what?

For example, it depends on the age of the cat. A kitten will need at least six feeding times per day at the beginning. I recommend feeding a fully-grown Sphynx at least three times a day. Other things to consider include your daily routine and the health of your cat.

Wild cats spend between 12 and 16 hours a day hunting and need to catch about 10 mice to satisfy their calorific needs. Their digestive system is designed to take frequent, small portions of food and not to eat a whole day's portion at once. Unfortunately, because housecats are dependent upon their owners to feed them, many have lost their natural rhythm. Eating too much at once can cause the stomach to overstretch, which can lead to your cat vomiting. If your cat often vomits after eating, it is a clear sign that the portions are too large.

Giving your cat free access to its food (for example with a food bowl which keeps refilling) does not represent the natural lifestyle of your cat. It usually leads to your cat taking in more calories than it uses during the day, resulting in it eventually becoming overweight. In reality, 50% of all cats in Germany are overweight, leaving them vulnerable to health problems. In addition, overweight cats can suffer from various disorders, such as Diabetes Mellitus, lameness or tumours. The life expectancy is reduced when the cat carries too much weight. As a result of gaining weight, your cat can also suffer from behavioural limitations: It will not be able to jump, hunt, play or explore as much. Over time this will result in your cat's inability to exhibit natural behaviour and can often lead to depression and extreme behavioural disorders.

I do not want to shock you, but it is important that you understand the problems which can face an overweight cat. For this reason, make sure that it does not build up unnecessary fat reserves and be sure to take your cat to the vet for regular examinations.

I solved the problem of the many small meals with my cats as follows: They get their regular meals in the mornings, midday and evenings. During the morning and late afternoons, I plan-in play, hunt and training units, during which my cats have to earn their food. This way, they take in five meals per day. The regular meals are mostly wet food, whereas the training rewards are usually made of dried food or special treats, like liver sausage. If you work full-time, and cannot work from home, you could ask if any of your neighbours would be willing to give your cat its food at lunchtimes.

I have one further tip for you. Try to feed it at the same time each day and in the same place. What do I mean by that? Cats love routines. They prefer their daily rhythm to be regular and love to know what will happen next.

Another important and underestimated aspect of feeding is the place. Unfortunately, some owners assume that their cats prefer to eat in quiet, secluded places, where they know they will not be disturbed. Of course, it is important that your Sphynx has peace while it is eating. There should be no children around, encouraging your cat to play or putting it under any pressure. Having said that, your cat would probably not like eating alone and completely isolated from the rest of the family. Choose a place where it can eat without being disturbed but also where it can be integrated into normal family life. Your cat likes to know what is going on and must also learn that it is ok if people get close to its food while it is eating. That may sound surprising, but cats which are used to eating alone can react very aggressively if people suddenly get close. You can avoid that from the beginning if you follow my tip.

My cats get their food at the same time as I eat my lunch or dinner. That has the advantage that I am already in the kitchen and at the same time the cats are distracted and are far less interested in what is going on at the dinner table.

Once your cat has finished eating, I suggest taking the plate away immediately – independent of whether there is still something in it or not. Why is this tip so helpful? This way you will get your cat used to eating all its food at once, which is useful if things have to move quickly.

Directly after they have eaten, I suggest a resting period. Your Sphynx should not run around or jump a lot for at least an hour after eating. There is no problem letting it out quietly into the garden to relieve itself. However, jumping round and running is not a good idea. Why? Your cat's stomach is very full after eating, and sudden movements could lead to it having a gastric torsion, which is deadly in 15% to 45% of cases. You will learn in Chapter 4 – "Common disorders" exactly what that is, how to recognise it and what to do if it happens.

Finally, it is better not to change over your cat's food too often. Every change could cause gastro-intestinal disorders. By changeover I am not only referring to a change from dry to wet food but also changing the tradename or type of food. Changing over the flavour of a product of the same type should not pose a problem and is even encouraged. You can offer your Sphynx flavour changes as much as you like. Offer it a variation of different tastes. Get your cat used to the fact that it will not get the same thing in its bowl every day from a very early age. The earlier it learns that food can taste differently, the less probability there is that it will refuse new food later on. If you want to change over your cat's food completely, you will need to do it in stages. Start slowly and substitute only a small portion of the old food with the new. You can slowly increase the amount until, after 3 to 4 weeks, you have completely changed over.

If your Sphynx is a poor eater, I suggest you check the temperature of its food. If the wet food, for example, is too cold because you have just taken it out of the fridge, or you have put cold water into the dry food bowl, your cat may not like it. Take care that the food you offer is room temperature (or mouse temperature, as I like to call it). It is better to let dry food soften for at least 10 minutes, so that its aroma can unfold and it is more digestible.

Often it is not the food itself which prevents cats from eating, but the bowl. It is very unpleasant for cats if their whiskers can touch the rim of the bowl while they are eating. It is better to serve the food on a flat plate or a wide bowl. There are some cats which do not like to eat out of metal or plastic bowls as it disturbs their delicate sense of taste. A glass or ceramic bowl seems to be the ideal solution there.

If, like me, you have more than one cat, make sure that there is enough distance between each food plate. It is important that each cat gets its own plate and all the cats do not have to eat out of one plate. The food fight would be pre-programmed and it is difficult for you to recognize if one of your darlings is not eating enough.

You should also not put the litter box too close to the feeding place. In most cases, either the cat will ignore the litter box (and find a better place somewhere in your home) or refuse to eat. Make sure to leave enough room when you are planning your home.

On the following pages, I have summarized the most important aspects which you need to consider when feeding your Sphynx.

Check list of feeding rules:

- ☐ Your cat should have at least three meals a day, more if possible, and you should always try to feed it at the same time in the same place.
- ☐ Ensure that your cat is not disturbed while it is eating, but the feeding place should not be out of eyeshot for your cat to see what is going on.
- ☐ Put the plate away after feeding, no matter whether there is still food on it or not.
- ☐ Keep to a quiet time of at least an hour after feeding.
- ☐ Do not unnecessarily change the make or type of food. If you have to change, you should do it slowly.
- ☐ Watch the temperature of the food. Cats find food which is too cold very unpleasant.
- ☐ It is better to use a plate or a wide bowl for feeding rather than a small bowl, preferably glass or ceramic.
- ☐ Every cat gets its own plate.
- ☐ Keep enough distance between the food place and the cat litter.

IF YOUR SPHYNX COULD DECIDE FOR ITSELF

All of today's house cats originate from wild cats. It is important for you to know this, so that you can understand your cat's nutritional needs and how to be consistent in providing them. The descendants of these wild animals are only genetically distinguishable from their ancestors by 0.1% to 0.3%! Would you have believed that?

What does this mean for you?

Wild cats only eat unprocessed meat (including offal, bones, fur etc.) and only eat plant foods if they have to. They gain 52% of their energy from the proteins, 46% from the fat and only 2% from the carbohydrates. Unfortunately, due to their meat-eating habits, cats have lost the ability to produce their own amino acids from their food. Therefore, it is essential for them to absorb the amino acids they need, such as taurine, arginine, methionine and cysteines through the meat they eat.

Did you know ...

... that cats do not eat grass because they want to eat plant foods, but to be able to vomit up the hair which they have swallowed during preening.

The myth that cats voluntarily eat plant-based food is therefore unfounded. The grass is regurgitated, together with the hair which your cat has swallowed, shortly after it has eaten it. If your cat is an indoor cat, I recommend always having a bowl of cat grass nearby for your cat to take if it needs it.

As a result, the cat's teeth are formed, mainly to rip meat into rough pieces. A grinding of food (e.g. grain-based) is not intended for their teeth and the same applies to the typical house cat of today.

Look carefully into the mouth of your Sphynx! It is very different from your own, which is not designed for ripping meat but more for grinding and chewing food. You will never see your cat grinding and chewing. It is much more likely to wolf down big pieces of food without even thinking of chewing it.

If you were to ask your Sphynx, it would instinctively (and genetically triggered) choose unprocessed meat which it could rip into pieces – happily with bones, fur and offal. This is particularly true of this beautiful breed, even if it no longer looks as much like its ancestors as some other breeds.

Sphynx cats love to spend time with their food. They enjoy ripping at a piece of meat and do not find it in the least tiresome, as we humans would do. As wild cats never know if their next hunting trip will be successful, they hunt, even if they are not hungry. Their instinct is programmed to ensure that their breed will continue to use its excellent hunting ability, which has been their most prominent selection characteristic for thousands of years. So, do not be surprised if your Sphynx enjoys a hunt, even after it has just eaten, that is in fact normal behaviour.

In the next chapter, you will discover what is on the cat's menu.

What is on the menu?

There are many differing opinions and many heated discussions about the correct nutrition for today's cats. There are avid proponents of every conceivable type of nutrition, as well as those who will not accept other people's opinions.

It really does not matter whether your cat is fed home-cooked food, BARF (only raw meat and vegetables), dry or wet food. I am sure that this comment will surprise many cat owners, but if we are honest, it is only logical that it is not important which method of feeding the owner uses, the important thing is that the cat is given enough to cover its nutritional and energy needs and that it takes in enough minerals, trace elements and vitamins. How it does that is really unimportant.

I will run over the most common methods of nutrition in the following pages. These are processed meals, BARF and home-cooked food. We will also touch on the subjects of vegetarianism and veganism.

You will discover what the pros and cons of each method of feeding are and what you need to watch with each one. In the last sub-chapter, we will look at what you need to do specifically for your Sphynx, compared to other breeds.

Did you know ...

... that fully-grown cats do not particularly like to eat things they do not know?

For this reason, it is advisable to get your Sphynx used to as many different tastes and consistencies as possible while it is still young. The more foods your cat knows, the less the probability that it will become a bad eater.

PROCESSED FOOD

Even though processed foods are often decried and demonised, I think I am not being presumptuous to assume that this form of food is the most common for today's house cat. In Germany alone, 435 million Euros was spent on dried food during 2018. This was only exceeded by wet food at a total of 473 million Euros and snacks at a value of 538 million Euros. All of these come under the heading of processed food. In total, the sum of more than 1.4 billion Euros changed hands over the counter during that period.

The enormous popularity of processed pet foods can be explained as follows:

- It is available everywhere.
- It is easy to store and quick to prepare.
- It is uncomplicated to calculate portion size.
- The preparation is carefully controlled by law and complies with the highest standards.
- Experts in nutrition have ensured that the food has the correct proportion of vitamins, minerals and trace elements, so that an animal is not under- or over-supplied with those substances.

In short: Processed food is practical! The owner does not need to worry about getting it right. However, few people know that processed food can normally be divided into three separate categories:

- Single feed: This is when the food is made up of a single component and is not meant to be fed to the animal on its own. One example is the non-mineralised meat tin.
- Feed Supplement: The food here is made up of at least two components but also these are not enough to ensure that your cat receives enough nutrients. Examples of this are cat snacks or a non-mineralised meat tin with vegetables. With a little practice, owners can create a balanced diet for their cats, using a mixture of single and supplement feed.
- Complete feed: As the name suggests, this food is enough by itself to cover the nutritional needs of your cat.

Unfortunately, there are some producers of complete feed who bend the statutory leeway very much to their own benefit, not always putting the health of the cat first, but rather their company profits. If you choose complete food, it is important that you check whether it is “good” food. I will explain what I mean right now: Take a packet of your present feed and we will look directly how good it really is.

Check first which type of feed it is. Is it single feed, feed supplement or complete feed? If, up to now, you have only been using single feed or feed supplement, it is possible that you have not been giving your Sphynx all the nutrition it needs. Next, check the list of ingredients. Interestingly, the ingredients of cat food do not legally have to be listed. If they are not openly and clearly declared, it could be a sign that not the best ingredients were used in the feed. Think about your choice of food. Do you not want to know exactly what is on your cat's menu? And why should the manufacturer not want to disclose the components of the food?

All other details about the analytical components of the cat food are, in my opinion, not very significant. Raw protein is meant to include both animal and plant proteins, which can vary wildly, not only in the quality but also in the digestibility of the food. Your Sphynx will tend to need more animal protein, but you will not be able to ascertain this from the packet.

Often, manufacturers use descriptions, such as "chicken flavour" on the packaging. Have you ever asked yourself how much "chicken" must really be in the food in this case? I will give you a short summary:

- **"Chicken flavour"**: In this case, there must be more than 0% but less than 4% of chicken in the food.
- **"Rich in chicken, extra chicken or with extra chicken"**: This describes a proportion of at least 14% of chicken which must be present in the food.
- **"Chicken Menu"**: This means that there must be at least 26% of chicken in the food.

Crude fibre, on the other hand, is an important information. Many people underestimate the importance of roughage (dietary fibre which is difficult or impossible to digest) in the consistency of your Sphynx's stools. It stimulates the bowel and helps it do its work. I, personally, have had very good results with crude fibre values of between 1.5% and 2%. If the value is too high (for example 4%), it could be damaging for your cat's bowel and can lead to flatulence. Apart from that, it says nothing about the quality of the food itself.

In my opinion, the crude fat value is as insignificant as the crude protein value, as it is not clear what kind of fat is meant.

One term which is often wrongly understood is the crude ash value. This is not referring to "ash" but to the inorganic components of your cat food. If the crude ash value is significantly above 15%, it could be a sign that, as an example, there are a lot of feathers and bones worked into the food. Of course, a wild cat can eat them without problem and they could contain useful minerals and trace elements. I doubt, however, that they need to be included in large amounts in processed food, but they offer a cost-effective alternative to nutritional muscle meat. Feed made from offal, which is offered as premium food, is always viewed sceptically, as there must also be a sufficient portion of muscle meat included in addition to the offal. A mouse would consist of about 11% of crude ash.

That was a very rough summary about what is contained in your cat's processed food, which you can see at first glance. As cats are meat eaters, I recommend that you take care that the carbohydrate value is as low as possible. Your cat needs neither sugar nor grain in its food. It can make the small amount of glucose that it needs by itself from amino acids. I believe a diet containing too much sugar and grain to be very dangerous; it can make your cat overweight and even sick. It is best to stay clear of any complete feed which contains either of these ingredients. My experience has shown that there is a high volume of grain contained in cheap, dry food.

It is important for you to pay special attention to the preparation and volume recommendations. Experts have put these ingredients together and have calculated how much of this food your cat needs. Make sure that your cat stays lean and do not overfeed it. After all, you know that overweight in cats can lead to behavioural abnormalities, which will deny your Sphynx from living a life suitable for its breed.

One closing tip for this chapter: It is best not to settle for a purely wet or dry diet, but give your cat a variety of both. If your cat is eating five meals a day, you will have the possibility to change the type of food around.

If you prefer to feed your cat single and supplement feed, I suggest asking an animal nutrition expert to calculate exactly what your Sphynx needs.

BARF

The trend towards healthy and natural nutrition has also not eluded cat owners. An increasing number of owners are trying to give their cat a natural diet, just like wild cats would eat.

In 1993, the BARF method of feeding was introduced by an Australian vet called Ian Billinghurst, who strongly recommended raw food for cats and dogs. BARF stands for Bone And Raw Food. Basically, it means feeding your cat raw food in a way acceptable to its breed.

This means, in effect, that your Sphynx only receives its nutrition from raw meat, offal, bones and fish. This is supplemented by fresh fruit, vegetables and nuts, which imitate the stomach contents of animals of prey.

I believe that the main advantage of using the BARF method is that you, the owner, know exactly what your Sphynx is eating and you know its quality. In processed food you only see the compressed pellets but you do not know what is in them. That means you have to rely on the specifications of the manufacturer.

Another, often underestimated, advantage is that the cat is occupied by eating for a longer period of time. It is often not possible for your cat to gulp down its food as in the case of most processed foods where the meat is cut into small pieces. In this case, cats must work for their food, with the effect that they become more active and well-balanced.

At this point I would like to discourage you from buying the BARF feeds which are available on the market. These have mostly been cut into smaller pieces and take away from the original purpose of the BARF method.

In most cases BARF food is better to digest, particularly for cats which have sensitive digestive systems or suffer from food intolerances. The following points are considered by many owners as positive side effects of BARF feeding, although they have not been proven:

- Improved immune system
- Fewer parasites
- Stronger bones
- Shiny fur

In addition to all these advantages there are also disadvantages to the BARF method, which could be serious for your Sphynx. The idea of feeding your cat naturally is wonderful, although it could lead to dangerous bacteria being in the food, parasites in raw meat or to an under or over supply of certain nutrients, if it is not done properly.

Salmonella bacteria have often been found in pre-packaged BARF products. Even though healthy cats with good immune systems are seldom affected by them, the cat's excrement infect their owners or other animals. To make sure that raw food does not contain parasites, I suggest using fresh meat from the butcher or, as an alternative, freezing the meat at -20°C for at least four days before feeding it. In that way, most of the parasites will be killed.

It is not easy to make a balanced, healthy feeding plan for your Sphynx and not many amateurs will be able to do it. In most cases, it leads to an under-supply of calcium together with an over-supply of phosphorous. Often there is also not enough Vitamin D, Taurine and Iodine in the food. In addition, too much muscle meat is not good for your cat either, as it could lead to kidney problems.

So, when someone asks me if I would recommend BARF feeding, I always answer: It depends!

As a Sphynx owner you need to be clear that this method of feeding will take up much more of your time than using processed food. The costs are also usually much higher. You will also need to work closely with a vet who is specialised in animal nutrition. You will be able to find a number of recipes on the internet but few of them would withstand scrutiny by an expert. No one who has not thoroughly examined your cat could give you a perfect recipe which includes all nutrients, minerals and vitamins which your Sphynx needs at any specific point in its life. Do not accept the promises of any online guru.

BARF feed? Yes, but if so, then correctly, and working together with an expert who is able to examine your cat regularly (preferably once a year). With the best will in the world, I cannot recommend a half-solution with shop-prepared feeds.

To give you an idea what a BARF meal looks like, I will give you an example for a 5kg active cat. Please do not use this as the only recipe for your Sphynx. An active and healthy Sphynx will receive 200g BARF, divided into the five meals mentioned previously. If your cat is a bit lazier, or a little older, you can reduce this amount to 150g:

- 115 g Muscle meat – beef or veal
- 21 g beef or veal heart
- 20 g beef or veal liver
- 20 g beef or veal stomach
- 21 g grated Zucchini (for valuable fibre)
- Approx. 4 chopped parsley leaves
- Salmon oil (delivers Omega 3 fatty acids and arachidonic acid)
- Powdered egg shell (delivers natural calcium)

As you can see, this recipe, is made up of a lot of components. It is better to make larger amounts of each in advance and to freeze them. I have found this to be useful and at the same time it reduces the quantity of bacteria and parasites which could be present. At the beginning, this form of feeding will take you a lot more time and commitment as simply feeding with processed food. With time, you will get faster as you get used to doing it. By then you will know what can be mixed with what and you may even be able to dispense with weighing everything, as you will have a feeling for the correct amounts. However, you must be clear from the start that it will always be extra work for you. In addition, if you travel several times a year, you need to be sure that your cat-sitter will be able to continue the BARF feed that your cat is used to.

HOME-COOKED FOOD

In principle, the situation with home-cooked food is similar to that of BARF feed. Here the cat owner also has full control over what his cat is given to eat. For this reason, it is important to discuss the exact composition of the feed with an animal nutrition expert.

In contrast to BARF feed, you will not give your Sphynx any raw meat, but you cook normal meals, which are prepared like those which humans eat. One important difference is that your Sphynx must not be given human food!

One of the reasons for this is that certain foods which humans eat are harmful, if not lethal, for your cat. Another is that the cat food will not contain any seasoning. As long as you keep to these principles, there is nothing to stop you from cooking for your Sphynx.

In general, the cat menu is similar to human food as it consists of meat, vegetables and a satiating ingredient, except that the distribution of it is different. When cooking, remember that your cat, unlike you, is not able to eat everything, but is basically a meat-eater. The following common components, however, may be included:

- **Meat:**

  Beef, poultry, lamb, rabbit and game are suitable. If you choose pork (or wild boar) you should make sure that the meat is cooked well through in order to avoid your cat getting stomach problems. In addition to muscle meat, you can add offal and organs (such as liver or heart). Be sure to get your meat from a reputable source in order to avoid contamination or rotten meat. You should avoid processed food (such as smoked meat or fish)

- **Fish:**

  Any kind of cooked fish is suitable for cats and they love it. Make sure you have removed all bones, or you could have a similar problem with your cat as can happen to humans. It is not recommended that your cat only eat fish instead of meat.

- **Eggs:**

  Eggs are a valuable source of protein and ensure that your cat has shiny fur. You can also use a small amount of the egg shell.

- **Milk/Milk Products:**

  Many cats cannot tolerate lactose, so there are only a few milk products which are suitable. Among them are curd cheese, sour milk and cottage cheese.

- **Potatoes/Rice/Carrots:**

  All three of these products can be used in home-cooked food but never without meat or fish.

- **Oil:**
  High quality oils should be used for preparing cat recipes. I suggest rapeseed, olive or fish oil.

- **Caution with Seasoning:**
  You should never use seasoning in cat food. This includes salt and pepper.

I would like to add here, that food types which are considered harmless to humans could not only harm our four-legged friends but even kill them. There is a summary of these harmful foods in Chapter 4 under “Poisons and problematic substances”.

When you are feeding your cat home-cooked food, it is important to include enough Taurine. As I already mentioned, unlike other animals, cats are not able to produce sufficient Taurine themselves and have to get this through their food (raw meat). Taurine is destroyed by heat, which means that it is no longer present in cooked meat, leading to your cat having a deficiency of it. You can buy Taurine commercially in powder form. You should always add this to the cooked meat you give to your cat. The amount you need is dependent upon the breed, age, weight and the other ingredients added to the cat feed and can vary enormously. It is best to consult an animal nutrition expert about the specific needs of your cat when feeding it BARF food. By the way, the mouse is the best supplier of Taurine for your cat – its natural prey.

I, personally, cook food for my cats for two, completely different reasons. The first is that I can make bland food for them if one of them is having gastrointestinal problems. For a few days, I will cook special food for it, which I will describe later in the book, then I know exactly what my cat's stomach has to work on. I also like to prepare snacks and treats myself, which I prepare in large amounts in advance and use as I need them.

The second reason is to spoil my cats. I have the feeling that I am doing something good for my cats when I cook for them. The 10 recipes which my cats like most have been added to the end of the book. I hope you will have as much pleasure from cooking them as I do.

VEGETARIANISM AND VEGANISM

It is not easy for vegetarians and vegans to deal with meat. For this reason, many people decide to feed their cats vegetarian food (meaning without meat) or even vegan (purely plant-based). The question of whether this form of nutrition is suitable for cats is extremely controversial.

If a cat owner decides on a vegetarian diet, this has seldom something to do with the health of the cat but is usually based on ethnic or religious principles of the human. For owners who want to form a close bond with their pets, the thought of intensive livestock farming or the slaughtering of animals is unbearable, and that is the reason why there are some who prefer to feed their cats vegetarian or vegan food.

The argument that this form of nutrition is not natural is weakened by the fact that this is also the case with tinned foods. Even the animal protection agency PETA supports feeding vegetarian food to cats. In the meantime, there are countless studies which recommend it and just as many studies which do not. As I mentioned at the beginning of this book, cats are not omnivorous, but meat eaters (also known as carnivores). Their digestive systems are formed to accept the majority of their food in the form of raw meat.

What should you do if you are unable to, or uncomfortable with feeding your Sphynx with meat?

In the first instance, perhaps you should reconsider whether a cat is the best pet for you. The question whether you should give your cat meat or not is not scientifically clarified as opinions and studies are extremely conflicting. However, there are enough different kinds of pets which have no problem in voluntarily eating vegetarian food. I would suggest to every staunch vegetarian not to get yourself a cat as a pet. In my opinion, you will not be able to give it the amount of important amino acids it needs. For me it seems to be a contradiction to give your cat its desperately needed amino acids, Taurine and vitamins through dietary supplements, when it is possible to give it what it needs in the natural way.

However, if you have definitely decided to get yourself a cat and want to feed it vegetarian or vegan food, please do this in close consultation with an animal nutrition expert. It is your responsibility to give your cat all the important minerals, trace elements, amino acids, Taurine and vitamins it needs. Form a plan, together with an expert, and make sure that you get the blood values of your Sphynx reviewed on a regular basis.

Something which I do not consider problematic at all is to feed your cat vegetarian food from time to time. My cat Sami loves bananas above everything and I sometimes give them as a snack. Sometimes I also leave out the meat part of the home-cooked food, but not always and also not most of the time.

Meat from controlled, animal test-free, organic sources could be an alternative to vegetarian food or tinned food, and can be fed using the BARF or home-cooked methods. At least then you can be sure that all these alternatives did not come from places practising intensive farming or animal cruelty.

I fully reject the idea of giving your cat a purely vegan diet and I will not discuss it any further in this book. I can only recommend such owners to choose a different pet in future, and not to choose a Sphynx.

WHAT YOU HAVE TO BE PARTICULARLY CAREFUL OF WHEN FEEDING YOUR SPHYNX

First the good news: In contrast to other breeds, the Sphynx does not exhibit any breed-typical intolerances or deficiencies. In principle, you do not have to pay attention to anything when feeding your cat that does not also apply to other breeds.

Due to its almost non-existent fur, your Sphynx will probably have a higher nutritional requirement than other cats of the same weight. Their bodies need more energy to keep their body temperatures constant, particularly in the colder seasons, meaning that they need to eat more.

How can you see whether your Sphynx is well nourished? A healthy Sphynx should have a flat, sinewy belly, and taut limbs with no fat on them. The fluff should be glossy and the eyes are awake and vigilant and your cat should always be ready for action. It is not normal for a Sphynx to be lazy and if it is, it can be a sign of incorrect nutrition.

Owners of the Sphynx in particular, prefer dry or wet food to any of the other alternatives, probably due to the easier handling and storage. BARFing and home-cooked food are of course also suitable for your Sphynx. Do not be surprised if it does not look very excited at the alternatives, if it has been used to eating processed food for years. The large amount of flavour enhancers contained in tinned food will make natural food taste too bland. You should stick with it and you will see that it will soon be eating its new food with enthusiasm.

When using food alternatives, it is important to pay attention to the quality and origin of the food. Any type of food is suitable, provided it contains all the necessary nutrition and your cat tolerates it well.

I always recommend that owners speak comprehensively with the breeder or the animal shelter about the nutritional needs of their new cat before they take it home. Ask about what it has been eating up to then and how to feed it over the coming weeks, especially if it is a kitten. Find out about the recommended form of nutrition for your cat. They know your new pet and its peculiarities and are often able to give you useful tips. It is often recommended to continue with the food your new pet is used to at the beginning. Any changes to that need to be carried out, very slowly and carefully.

THE WATER INTAKE OF YOUR CAT

There is much discussion about the correct feeding method and the right quality of food. However, there is something which your cat needs much more than food: Water!

If it had to, your cat could survive weeks without food, but only a few days without water. On the following pages, I will explain how you can determine the water requirement of your Sphynx and how you can motivate your cat to drink, if it is not doing so by itself.

Did you know, ...

... that you should not offer your Sphynx milk instead of water? Most adult cats do not tolerate milk very well! You can serve your cat lactose-free milk or cat milk which some manufacturers praise highly, but you should know that they represent a high-calorie snack and are not a substitute for water.

THE WATER REQUIREMENT OF YOUR SPHYNX

Your Sphynx will not live long without drinking enough water, as water is necessary for a number of physiological functions. Water, for example, is necessary to dissolve food components in the intestines and transport it through the blood vessels to the muscles and organs, to flush toxins out of the kidneys and to regulate its body temperature.

As you can see, countless functions are reliant upon your cat having enough water. Generally, cats can take in water in three ways:

1. Through actively drinking: Your cat will take the majority of its water requirement this way and it is the most obvious method.

2. Through its food: Cats take in water through their food. The amount varies greatly, depending on whether your cat eats wet or dry food. BARF-fed cats in particular take in the majority of their daily water requirement through the fresh food.

3. Through their metabolism: It may sound strange, but some of your cat's water needs are provided through the metabolic process.

It is important that you keep the water supply to your Sphynx as regular as possible, so that all its physiological functions can work properly. It is not good if your cat has to take in all its requirement at one time, as this can lead to deficiency symptoms and your cat will most probably be very thirsty in between. Make sure that it always has access to fresh water whenever it needs it.

The water source should always be clean and if it is kept in a water bowl, I recommend cleaning it regularly. You should clean the bowl using washing-up liquid or vinegar essence at least once a week. Please ensure that any detergent residue is removed so that your Sphynx does not digest it. When going for a walk[3] I suggest taking water with you for your cat to drink. Of course, it can drink out of puddles or pools, but standing water can often contain germs or pathogens and is not really advisable. Some ponds are real incubators for bacteria. Flowing water which appears clean, on the other hand, can be drunk without hesitation in most countries.

Germany's tap water is also unproblematic to use. However, if it is strongly chlorinated because of its germ load, many cats will not drink it because they do not like the way it tastes. If this occurs - it is mostly only for a few weeks - you can change over to still mineral water for that period. The carbonates in sparkling water are not harmful

---

[3] If you want to learn how to take your Sphynx for a walk on the lead, I recommend reading the second part of this series, „Training a Sphynx Cat". More information can be found at the end of this book.

for your cat as such, but they can lead to stomach problems and flatulence. I have heard some owners say that their cats completely refuse to drink tap water. This does not necessarily have to be due to the water itself, but can also be due to the water pipes. If this happens, there is not much else you can do but give your cat mineral water regularly. Make sure that the water is always room temperature, also in the summer. If it is too cold, it can irritate its stomach and lead to vomiting or diarrhoea. Most cats also refuse to drink water if it is too warm.

A healthy Sphynx loses liquid in many different ways during the day. This can be via the faeces, via the urine, via the respiratory tract, via the skin and, in the case of lactating cats, also via the teats. The amount of water each cat needs depends on various factors. Among them are the cat's weight, the previously mentioned water loss, the ambient temperatures, the amount of physical activity and the type of food it eats. Three quarters of the amount a cat needs can be covered by eating wet food.

To help you to get a feeling for how much your Sphynx needs to drink each day, you can use the following rule of thumb:

A fully-grown Sphynx which is fed with wet food and lives at a normal room temperature around 20 degrees Celsius, weighing an average amount, needs about 55 to 65 ml water per kilogram of its body weight. With a cat of 5kg, this makes a water requirement of 275 to 325 ml.

If your cat is more active or if the ambient temperature increases, the amount of water your cat needs, increases accordingly. The same applies to salty food. As with us humans, this leads to an increase in water requirement. Now you have the rule of thumb, you see that there is a certain amount of leeway. Anything which is far below or far above that average should be checked by a vet, as too much or too little water requirement could be a sign of an ailment.

If your Sphynx comes within the amount of leeway mentioned above, there should be no problems, provided your cat is behaving normally. If you pay particular attention to your cats drinking habits for a few weeks you will notice how much it needs in normal circumstances and how much difference a higher temperature makes to its thirst. As usual, every cat needs to be treated as an individual.

HOW TO MOTIVATE YOUR SPHYNX TO DRINK

Generally, healthy cats will always drink enough water for their needs, provided they have access to it as, - contrary to us humans – they listen carefully to what their body says.

However, it can happen that a physically healthy cat does not drink enough. One reason could be the hot temperature in the summer, when your Sphynx needs to drink a lot more water than it is used to. Stress can also have a negative effect on your cat's behaviour when it comes to drinking. Just like we humans, a cat could stop eating and drinking due to stress.

Below you will find a few tips how you can motivate your cat to drink enough water:

- Add more water to your cat's food than usual. You can substitute wet food for dry food, so that your cat automatically takes in more water. You would not normally add extra water to wet food but in this case, I suggest trying it.
- Add a little taste to the water. You can try meat stock, liver sausage or sausage water, but you must be careful not to make the water too salty.
- Add some fruit to the water: Cranberries or bilberries for example. That way you make the drink more interesting and many cats play with

the fruit in the water and try to fish it out. They will automatically take in more water in the process.

- Think about purchasing a water dispenser or drinking fountain. Some cats drink more if they are offered flowing water.

If your Sphynx still refuses to drink enough water, or none at all, despite all your efforts, and is generally not behaving as it usually does, it will be better to consult a vet. It is possible that your cat has some kind of disorder and you need to find out what to do.

On the following pages, you will find a checklist which contains all the things you need to know about the drinking behaviour of your Sphynx.

... that you should not place your cat's water bowl next to its feed plate?

In the wild, cats do not have a water bowl near their freshly caught mouse, but have to find water themselves. Most cats have retained that habit to this day. Put the water bowl or drinking fountain in another place within your home, and not next to the feed plate.

Drink behaviour checklist:

- ☐ Always ensure that your Sphynx has enough water available.
- ☐ Make sure that the water is room temperature and does not contain carbon dioxide, so that your cat does not suffer from stomach problems.
- ☐ Clean the water bowl regularly.
- ☐ Your cat should avoid drinking from standing water when you are outside with it. Take fresh water with you when you go out.
- ☐ Increase the amount of water you provide when your cat has been very active or if the outside temperature is increasing.
- ☐ Offer water with meat stock, liver sausage or sausage water to motivate your cat to drink.
- ☐ Soften dry food in sufficient water and add extra water to wet food.
- ☐ Do not put the water bowl next to the food plate, but find another place for it in your home.

- Consult a vet if your cat refuses to drink water and appears exhausted, tired and lacking motivation.

- Chapter 3 -

THE BASICS OF GROOMING

It is a normal part of our daily routine to practise personal care. However, many people do not take the same care about their cats. I would even dare to say that most cat owners do not believe that they have to take much care of their cat's hygiene, if at all, and that the cats do all the important things themselves.

In principle this assumption is not completely wrong. However, there are great differences regarding this from breed to breed. When you got your Sphynx, you chose a breed which needs very little body care compared to a Turkish Angora, for example. However, you must be aware that even with a Sphynx there are certain things that you need to take care of.

If your Sphynx is not used to being examined and groomed from a very young age, it is advisable to start off very gently. Do not begin with the full programme that you will read about in this book. Start with a very short examination, but repeat it several times a day, to condition your cat to it. Try to make the examination and the care programme as pleasant as possible for your cat and use treats, cuddles and praise if your Sphynx remains calm and behaves as you want it to.

The main thing is that you yourself remain calm. Even if your cat is twisting and resisting, you must remain calm and composed. Once you have mastered that, your calmness will eventually transfer over to your cat. If you react to your cat's behaviour, and become nervous or even annoyed, you will only achieve the opposite. Your cat's nervousness will grow and it will learn to hate the regular examinations, thus programming regular stress and conflict for the next few years. It is better to remain calm, no matter what your Sphynx does!

Again, I strongly suggest: Begin in small steps and do not overstress your Sphynx. Every small step taken with certainty is far more valuable than a hasty big step marked by uncertainty.

I am often asked why it is necessary to go to such trouble, as today's house cats are descendants from wild cats which did not have anyone to look after and groom them. This sounds like a reasonable argument at first sight, but does not withstand a closer look.

In contrast to the wild cat, which can reproduce freely, today's domestic cats are deliberately bred and therefore have certain characteristics that Darwin believed would probably not have prevailed in the wild. Humans have had a major impact on how each breed evolved, thereby promoting certain traits that deserve special attention, such as the small gene pool and sensitivity to cold of your Cornish Rex.

In addition, the lifestyle of today's housecats is vastly different from that of a wild cat. Through their co-existence with humans, they have become dependent upon us for things such as their intensive grooming needs, for example.

There are also other aspects, such as the fact that your home stays much cleaner if you brush your Sphynx regularly. Instead of losing its hair slowly, like the wild cat does, you help it to lose its hair quicker by brushing it and at the same time you minimise the cat hairs which fly around in your home.

As already mentioned, when choosing your Sphynx, you chose a breed which does not need much grooming. However, I will explain to you on the following pages how to regularly examine the eyes, skin, fur, ears, teeth and paws of your Sphynx. If you stick to the routine, you and your cat will feel better in the long run and you will be able to recognise possible disorders early, before they become acute.

The following tips are based on the opinions of vets, specialised literature and other experts. If you keep all the suggestions, you will be spending many hours with the examination and grooming of your cat. You will probably suspect all kinds of disorders and dangers for your four-legged friend – I do not wish that upon you. On the next pages, you will be confronted by many problems, which could happen to your Sphynx. The important word here is "could" – that does not mean that they will happen and certainly not altogether.

You will be fine if you just use your common sense. If your cat has already had problems with its eyes, you will need to keep a closer watch on them than you would with other cats with healthy eyes. If you do not find anything conspicuous, then do not stress your cat with unnecessary, daily examinations and care programmes, but rather extend the time between the examinations. Do what is necessary well, and leave everything which is not necessary alone.

At the end of each chapter, I will give you a recommendation as to what I think is important with my cats and what I believe to be less significant. Please do not blindly follow my recommendations, but take into account the needs and problems of your own Sphynx. Every cat is different and has different needs. However, with my help and recommendations I hope to help you to consider your situation with the same moderation.

Eye care

Our little kitties have us firmly in their grip with their saucer eyes. We want them to stay that way so it is important that you have them examined regularly. Many experts and vets recommend that you check your cat's eyes every day, particularly if they are allowed outside.

Healthy cat eyes are clear and shiny. The lids lie close to the head and are clean. There is no mucus or incrustations on them. If your cat has slightly dried teardrops in its eye after a long rest, that is normal and is similar to the sleeping dust which we humans often have in our eyes.

To examine them, you should hold your Sphynx's head gently in your hands and stroke its fur to the side. If you notice that your cat often suffers from sleeping dust in its eyes, you can run a damp cloth gently over its eyes every morning after it gets up to remove it. Be careful not to use a fluffy cloth as you do not want the fluff to go in its eyes. Use a separate cloth for each eye, so that any pathogens are not transferred from one eye to the other.

If your cat often has problems with its eyes, you can dip your cloth into lukewarm saline solution, or camomile tea. You should filter the water before use so that there is no residue which can get into your cat's eyes.

If the hair around the eyes of your Sphynx is too long, it is a good idea to trim it regularly. That way you avoid dirt getting into its eyes from the long hair, or the hair itself causing irritation.

The following symptoms could be a sign that there is something wrong with your cat's eyes and you should consult a vet:

- Above average sensitivity to light
- Touching its eyes with its paws
- Sensitivity to touch
- Thick discharge from the eye
- Badly bloodshot eyes
- Enlarged pupils
- Any changes to the eyes.

In addition, it is advisable to protect your cat's eyes from unnecessarily large amounts of dust and pollen. Sometimes it is worth considering keeping an outside cat indoors for a while, particularly if it often suffers from eye problems. Leave your cat inside for a few days. If your cat still has problems, you can rinse out its eyes with a mild eye cleaning liquid without preservatives after it comes back in from the outside. You can get such eye cleaning liquid from the pharmacy or pet shop. Dry air can be just as problematic as dust or pollen. Just like humans, cats can get burning or runny eyes from the dry air caused by the heating system.

In contrast to us humans, the cat does not know the reason for it and will not stay clear of the fireplace of heaters. If you notice that your Sphynx often suffers from runny eyes or often blinks, particularly in the colder seasons, again a damp cloth with camomile will do the trick. Get into the habit of putting a bowl of water onto the heaters or near the fireplace, to increase the amount of humidity in the air. It will not only help your cat's eyes but yours too.

Just as cats do not know the danger of dry heat, they also do not realise that draughts can be harmful. On the contrary, many cats love to lie in the draught and deliberately lean head towards it. Take care that your cat does not often get the opportunity to do that, as it can lead to conjunctivitis.

My recommendation for you!

If your Sphynx does not suffer from problems with its eyes, it is not necessary to check them every day. I have not needed to do regular checks of my cat's eyes up to now and also never needed to remove morning dust from its eyes. That does not mean that my cat does not have any morning dust, but that it has always cleared up by itself. If I notice anything, I keep an eye on my cat to make sure that it does not get worse and do not do anything for the time being.

You should definitely consider my tips about draughts and dry air. It does not take much effort, but it can save your cat a lot of suffering.

SKIN AND COAT CARE

Generally, a cat's fur is a mirror of its health. If its fur is shiny, dense and resilient, you can assume that your Sphynx is healthy. As soon as its fur changes, it becomes dull and brittle, matted or seems to be falling out in large amounts, there can be a problem. Mostly the problem is just below the fur – often such problems occur through skin irritation. Other causes could be a nutrition deficiency or parasites.

Not only is the skin the biggest organ of your cat, it fulfils several important tasks:

- **It protects your cat from pathogens.** It serves as an immunological boundary and keeps bacteria, fungi and other harmful substances away from the inner organs.
- **It regulates the temperature of your cat.** The expansion and contraction of the blood vessels protect your cat from heat and cold.
- **It supports communication.** Tiny muscles in the skin cause the fur to stand on end. In addition, both fragrances and hormones are released through the skin.

- **It helps to detoxify.** Breakdown products from metabolism and other harmful substances can be ejected through the skin.
- **It is responsible for the fur change.** The hair follicles which make up your cat's coat are within the skin of your cat. Twice a year, the fur change will take place, starting from that point.

Regular fur care and a balanced diet are necessary to ensure healthy skin and beautiful fur. What many owners do not know is that the first signs of deficiencies usually show up in the skin and fur.

Now you may be wondering what the healthy skin of your Sphynx should actually look like? Is it red, dry or flaky or is your cat scratching a lot? These could all be signs of a skin disorder. The same applies to a dull or greasy coat or loss of fur generally.

Experts suggest grooming the skin and fur every day, or at least to examine them. The whole thing does not have to become a boring routine, but can be a cherished ritual through intensive contact, which strengthens your relationship with each other.

In fact, brushing your Sphynx takes very little time. Regular care ensures that significantly less hair or skin particles come off than if you only do it irregularly. At the same time, you can remove all the dirt which your cat collected while it was out in the garden, before it can spread throughout your home. Additionally, you will find any ticks, fleas or other parasites much quicker.

Naturally, your Sphynx is well able to take care of its own thin fur by licking it, which it does on most days anyway. However, this does cause your Sphynx to swallow a lot of fur, which then turns into hairballs, which are later ejected through vomit. I do not know how you look at it but I prefer to find as few hairballs as possible in my home, so I declared regular brushing to be a vital part of my cats' wellness programme, right from the beginning. As the owner of a Sphynx cat, the fur-care programme is happily much easier than with other breeds.

If your Sphynx is not used to regular brushing and reacts uneasily or even aggressively to it, I offer you the same advice as with the eye care: Take it steadily and sweeten it with a lot of treats and cuddles. Make brushing a pleasant experience for your cat, which it looks forward to. Begin by playing with your cat and tiring it out. The more relaxed it is after the play session, the less upset and aggressively it will react to being brushed. When your Sphynx has recovered from its game and is calm and relaxed, you can reward it with a few extra cuddles until you take up the brush without it noticing. I suggest using a baby hair brush, or alternatively, a nopped glove, which doubles up to become a massage item. Be sure always to brush in the direction from the ears to the tail. You should never comb the tail, but brush it gently. When brushing the belly, it is simplest to brush from the back to under the belly with a standing cat, rather than try to encourage it to lie on its back.

When you chose your Sphynx, you picked a breed that is easy to groom. It naturally has hardly any hair. Grooming will not take as long as with long-haired breeds.

You should not bathe your Sphynx, except if it becomes very dirty or is absolutely necessary due to an illness. Intensive bathing, and in particular shampooing, destroys the fur's natural protection and grease layer of the skin. That can lead to skin irritation and itchiness. Only bathe your cat in exceptional circumstances and only use shampoo if it is absolutely necessary.

In addition, most cats hate water and you must be prepared for it to offer resistance. In preparing for the bath, I suggest using a small bath tub with an anti-slip mat. A normal bath tub is not a good choice as there are too many ways for your cat to escape. Make sure that the water is warm but not hot. The room should be nice and warm, so that your Sphynx does not get cold while its fur is wet.

Did you know...

... that you should never use human shampoo? The skin of your Sphynx has a different PH-value than that of humans. It does not tolerate human shampoo, and if used regularly, can cause skin irritation. You will be able to find shampoo specifically for cats in every well-stocked pet shop.

Take it very easy during the first bath. Begin by wetting your cat's paws, one at a time. If your Sphynx stays calm and relaxed you can start on the legs. Go slowly over the body towards the front. Continue along the tail, the sides and the back.

Only wet your cat's head when it is used to bathing or when it is completely relaxed. If it is not, I suggest using a wet sponge or washcloth to go over its head. Do not shampoo its head, to avoid getting shampoo in the eyes, ears, muzzle or nose. Be just as gentle when rinsing your cat.

If your Sphynx begins to panic, stop immediately. There is no point in continuing if your cat is not feeling well. Try to calm it down with treats and cuddles and next time make sure that your cat is powered-out with a playtime before you start. You must remain calm and do not get angry, stressed or annoyed.

When you are finished with bathing, try to dry your cat straight away, as best as you can. Do not rub too hard. Many cats do not like the hairdryer. You could try it because it is the quickest way to get your cat dry. However, if your Sphynx does not like it, you should stop. In winter, you must take particular care that the room is warm enough after bathing your cat, until it is completely dry, to avoid it getting a cold. In summer, when it is warm, you can leave out the towel-drying and hairdryer completely, as your cat will enjoy its cool, damp fur. As wet cats are very sensitive to draughts, you should ensure that all windows and doors are closed until your Sphynx is completely dry.

You may use care products, such as sprays, but they are not necessary. If your cat is well nourished, its fur will shine well enough without them.

My recommendation for you is:

I rarely carry out a separate examination of the fur or skin as it is not necessary. It is a tradition of ours to have a long cuddle every evening, which enables me to take a good look at the skin and fur at the same time. I am flexible about brushing. In principle I brush my pet several times a week, but I use the nopped to give my cat a nice massage. In addition, it gets an extra round of brushing if it has come back very dirty after a long, rainy adventure in the garden, which luckily does not happen all that often.

I usually wait until my cats are dry then brush the dirt out of their fur, to avoid having to bathe them. This may be a solution for you too if your cat does not suffer from chronic skin, fold or fur problems.

EAR CARE

I do not need to stress how important your Sphynx's ears are. They are not only used for hearing, but also for balance and communication with others of its kind. Experts therefore also recommend regular ear checks.

The cat's ear is composed of three parts:

- The outer ear
- The middle ear
- The inner ear

Cats can hear much better than you or I and they can also perceive frequencies that are higher and lower than what we can hear.. As you want it to stay that way, regular examination of your cat's ears is essential.

Ideally, you will not detect anything in particular, as a healthy cat ear is well supplied with blood and will appear clean. Cat's bodies are able to clean themselves. For example, it will produce enough ear wax to clear out the dirt, fine protective hairs keep dust and other particles out before they can enter the inner ear and good ventilation does the rest to defend against the moist, warm climate, which favours bacteria.

The most common ear disease of the cat is disorders of the outer ear and the outer ear canal. The following symptoms could suggest that something is wrong:

- You detect a strange and unpleasant smell coming out of the ears.
- The ear canal is very dirty or clogged (for example with a black secretion or ear wax).
- You detect small black spots in the ear (possibly parasites).
- You see reddening or even pus (Warning – this could be an infection).
- You find a fresh wound or bleeding.
- You notice that your Sphynx is scratching its ears a lot, often shaking its head or holding its head askew.

In the case of most of these symptoms, it is advisable to consult a vet to find out what the cause could be. If there is only light soiling of the outer ear, you can try to clean it yourself.

For that I would recommend a moist, fluff-free cloth, which you can wrap around your finger and gently clean the ear. It is important that the cloth is not too damp and that no liquid drips into the inner ear. Make sure that you dry the outer ear thoroughly when you are finished. Any dampness which is left could cause bacteria to breed. If you want, you can use camomile tea instead of water as this has an anti-inflammatory effect. You should ensure that the liquid, whether water or tea, is at room temperature.

If the ear is very dirty, you can purchase a cleaning lotion and drops from the pet shop. If you choose to do that, you should do it outside or in the bath tub as your cat will want to shake vigorously after treatment. If the symptoms do not disappear quickly, it will be advisable to consult a vet.

You should never use cotton ear buds to clean your cat's ears. There is a great danger that you will push germs, dirt or wax deeper into the ear, causing enormous damage. It is also possible that your cat will make an unexpected movement with its head, leading to irreparable damage to the eardrum.

Finally, I would like to mention: Similar to the eye and coat care, you should get your Sphynx used to ear care from a very early age. Take it slowly and link the examination and any cleaning necessary to the reward of cuddles and the odd treat.

My recommendation for you is:

As the self-cleaning function in the ears of your Sphynx is impaired due to the lack of hair around the ears, it is advisable to examine them regularly and if necessary to clean them with a cotton wool pad. I often take a look at my cat's ears but I only clean them if I see that they are very dirty. If you have an outside cat, you need to pay more attention to its ears as parasites can appear more frequently during specific seasons. If your Sphynx has not had any previous problems with its ears, you will probably get along well with this routine, too.

TOOTH CARE

Tooth care is a matter of course for us humans, but many cat owners think that it is not necessary for their pets. That is wrong. Your cat's teeth are used for communication, as a hunting weapon and an eating tool, it is even more important for them to be – and remain - in good condition. You will learn how to do that in this chapter.

Just like humans, your Main Coon has milk teeth at the beginning of its life. These fall out in between their third and sixth month, which often causes your kitten to gnaw at everything in sight. Your cat does this too speed up the painful process of the tooth change. An adult cat has 30 teeth, which it uses to grab, hold, rip, kill and eat. Ideally, you should get your cat used to you regularly examining its gums and teeth, right from the start. If you notice that the teeth are a light yellow-brown colour or that there are brown edges to the gums, this can be an alarm signal. It is most probably plaque or a bacterial infection. If your cat's breath also has an unpleasant smell, this is also a strong sign that it may have tooth problems or an infection of its gums. This also includes bloody or red gums.

It is better not to wait until it happens, but to be proactive, and, with the correct tooth care, you can prevent it from happening altogether. Statistically about 75% of all cats over three years of age suffer from some form of impairment in the mouth – a shockingly high number, which shows how important prevention is.

The most common cause of plaque is usually the wrong food, or food which is caught between the teeth, causing bacteria to collect. The minerals in the saliva turn the food rest to tartar, which can only be removed by a vet.

Toothcare in cats always begins with their food. Cats who are only fed softened dried food or wet food, do not get the chance very often to chew or rip their food. They are able to swallow the small, soft pieces of food directly. In contrast, cats who are fed muscle meat have to chew much more, depending on the size of the pieces – and this is exactly where natural tooth care begins.

Chewing (or ripping) cleans the surface of your Sphynx's teeth automatically and prevents plaque, and later tartar, to develop. The increase in the saliva flow also adds to the cleaning effect. This procedure is most effective when your cat is given unsoftened dry food or even fresh meat in addition to its wet food. The hard, dried food will automatically clean the plaque off the teeth. There is even dry food which has been formulated specifically to clean teeth.

... that active cats have much fewer problems with their teeth?

Scientific studies have shown that the flow of saliva increases while your cat is being active, which leads to better tooth hygiene.

Chew toys or special chew articles from the pet shop are a good addition to natural tooth care. A cat's teeth can also be given a thorough clean with special cat toothbrushes and cat toothpaste. However, I would only recommend that if your cat has a misalignment of its teeth which makes them inaccessible. It is best to get your cat used to the procedure when it is still a kitten so that it will put up with you later.

My recommendation for you is:

You should have no trouble getting a healthy Sphynx used to dry and wet food. Take extra care that your cat only receives unsugared feed. Feeding a lot of treats in between meals can also accelerate the speed at which plaque appears. If your cat does not have any prior sicknesses, you do not need to examine its gums and teeth each day – now and again is enough. However, if your Sphynx refuses to eat or has a strong mouth odour, I recommend taking a closer look at its teeth.

What applies to humans also applies to our cats: The older you are, the more vulnerable your teeth and gums become. The older your Sphynx is, the sooner you will notice plaque on its teeth. I can only suggest adjusting the time between the examinations to suit the age of your cat.

PAW CARE

Many people believe that giving your cat a pedicure is excessive behaviour – however I, as well as many experts and vets, see it differently. Perhaps you have noticed that your Sphynx licks its paws or chews its claws. If that is the case, your cat urgently needs a pedicure. This is not a cosmetic measure, but important care in order to avoid great health problems in the future.

But, why is it necessary? After all, wild cats, even today, do not need pedicures. Instead, nature takes care of the important paw care for them. This is largely due to the fact that the wildcat has been running over hard surfaces, rocks and stones since kitten age, so it can find opportunities to sharpen its claws everywhere.

It is different with housecats of today. They are mostly within our own four walls, where we really do not like them scratching. In addition, they are subject to additional exposures, such as road salt, which its wild cousins do not have to worry about.

Cat's claws are unique. No other animal is able to extend or retract its claws when it wants. This is made possible by the relaxing or tensing of additional tendons, enabling the cat to retract its claws into special pockets of skin on its paw and extend them again when it wants to. For this reason, the cat does not wear out its claws by walking, as they are normally withdrawn. They only extend them again when climbing or scratching and then they will become worn down. Having a cat tree in your home is essential to avoid you having to cut your cat's claws with tiresome regularity.

Let us have a look at how you will know that your Sphynx needs paw care:

- Your cat will get caught on the carpet while walking.
- Your cat keeps licking or nibbling its paws.
- Your cat scratches itself while cleaning its fur.
- Your cat puts its paws down at a light angle when walking.

If you notice any of these signs, it is high time to check your cat's paws. Besides that, experts recommend that you check your cat's paws at least once a week, or after it has been outdoors.

While examining the paws, check if dirt has collected between the pads or under the claws. If so, you should remove it. If the hair between the pads is so long that it clearly shows through, you should cut it. For one thing, the hair can collect more dirt and little stones, which can be painful. For another, the hair can mat very quickly and cause your cat to slide on slippery surfaces. I recommending using a pair of scissors with rounded ends for cutting the hair. If the paws are very dirty, a lukewarm paw bath can also be helpful.

If you notice cracks, cuts or even in-growing claws while examining your cat's paws, it is advisable to consult with a vet. In the first instance, you can treat them with an oily cream or Vaseline (particularly with cracked pads) but I would still recommend having your vet take a look at them, particularly when it is beginning to happen more often. In both cases, camomile tea as a paw bath is very effective.

During wintertime, you need to pay particular attention to the paws if yours is an outside cat. Grit, ice and salt can be very harmful for them. During the colder periods, you should get used to checking your cat's paws after every trip outdoors. In addition, I cream my cat's paws with Vaseline each time before it goes outside. If your cat is particularly prone to sore and cracked paws during the warmer seasons, you may want to think about purchasing cat shoes for the winter. Make sure that they fit well, are of good quality and cannot be pulled off by your cat. Alternatively, perhaps you could think whether it is worth letting your cat go outdoors at all if it has such problems, or whether you should restrict its outdoor trips to the balcony or garden.

Now we are coming to the claw care itself: Cutting claws is something that nearly everyone can do. However, I recommend asking your vet to show you how to do it the first time. There are nerves and blood vessels which run through the claw, called the "quick". You must never damage this part as it is very painful for your cat and it bleeds a lot too.

Never rely on a spacer claw cutter, but check for yourself how much you can cut. I recommend working with a lot of light underneath the paw. This way you can better see where the quick lies. Sometimes it helps to place a torch underneath the claw, so you can see it better.

It is very important that your cat remains quiet, while you are clipping its claws, and does not try to pull its paw away. One tip I can offer you is to tire-out your Sphynx before you start, thus increasing the possibility that it will stay still. Do not hold the paw too loosely. Remember when clipping the claw to make the experience as pleasant as possible. You can do that by offering it treats and giving it a lot of cuddles.

Practise putting light pressure on your cat's pads, and the top of its paw. This will cause the claw to be pushed out a little. Cut only the dead part of the claw. As soon as you notice that the dead part is all gone, stop immediately. The technique is to hold the cutters vertically and always cut at a right-angle to the direction of growth of the claw. Never cut more than a millimetre at a time, so that you do not cut too far. If you stay calm during the whole process it will give your cat support. Do not over-tire it but do give it a lot of praise when you are finished.

If you do happen to cut into the quick, you should remain calm. It will look worse than it is because of the heavy bleeding. Hold a cotton wool pad or compress onto the wound with some pressure and wait a few minutes. Normally the bleeding will have stopped by then. If it has not, you could try an old household remedy. Mix some flour with a little water to make a thick stodge. Press this onto the wound with a cotton wool pad or compress for a few minutes. The stodge will clump together and form a kind of plug onto the wound.

If the bleeding has not stopped after about 20 minutes, you should consult a vet. If it has stopped, you can bandage it and cover the whole paw with an old (but freshly-washed!) sock. You can secure it with some sticky tape so that your Sphynx cannot bite it off, or rip it. The sock is there so that the fresh wound does not get infected and should be left in place for about a week. Inspect the wound daily. As long as nothing is inflamed, and your cat is behaving normally, a visit to the vet is not necessary in my opinion. Another alternative is to treat the wound with a blood-staunching stick, which you can buy in any pharmacy where you can find shaving materials.

As I said before, claw care is not difficult but it needs to be done carefully, with a sure hand and a lot of patience. For beginners, it can be difficult to see where the quick starts. In that case it is advisable to ask a professional – in this case your vet – to show you how to do it. However, if you do feel confident enough after that, you can do it yourself. Otherwise, you can continue to get it done at your vets.

My recommendation for you is:

I do not think that it is necessary to check your cat's paws much, except during the winter months. In winter, the salt, road grid and ice have often caused wounds or cracks on my cat's paws which I have treated with Vaseline.

Right from the beginning I have enthusiastically rewarded my cats when they have used the cat tree. Because of that, I hardly have any problems with long claws. I must admit, that I do not like cutting their claws myself and usually have them done at the vet, but I do know many cat owners who are able to cut the claws of their cats themselves without any problems.

WHAT YOU NEED TO PAY PARTICULAR ATTENTION TO WHEN GROOMING YOUR SPHYNX.

You have learned a lot about grooming your Sphynx in the previous pages. I think it is important here to stress that you do not have to carry out the full programme every day. Watchful cat owners, who engage with their cats every day, plays, hunts, trains and cuddles with them, will normally not need to make specific examinations to notice changes in them. However, I urge you to train your Sphynx to understand that it is alright for you – or your vet – to examine its paws, ears, eyes and teeth. Doing that will save you, and anyone else involved, much anguish, distress and hassle.

I am sure that there are many Sphynx cats which can live long and happy lives without this care from their owners. However, there are also many which suffer silently and no one notices. In your cat's interests, you should invest this relatively short amount of time. The best part of it is: Not only will this improve the health of your Sphynx, but will also strengthen the bond between you, too. The intensive examinations, and the high degree of trust which your cat puts in you, will bring you even closer together.

Check List: Regular Grooming

The following is true of healthy Sphynxs:

- ☐ The eyes are clear and shiny. They show no signs of redness, mucus or other changes.
- ☐ The skin is not reddened, dry or flaky.
- ☐ Its folds are clean, dry and free of parasites.
- ☐ The fur is shiny and dense. There is not much hair loss out of the moulting time.
- ☐ The ears are not dirty, red or have dark spots and your cat is not shaking its head or scratching its ear more than usual.
- ☐ The teeth do not have a yellow-brownish coating on them and the gums are neither red nor bleeding. Your cat does not have an unpleasant mouth odour.
- ☐ The paws are not cracking or sore, neither is there any dirt between the pads
- ☐ Your cat does not get stuck on the carpet when walking over it or on cloth covers.

Check List: Grooming Utensils

I recommend the following utensils for grooming your Sphynx:

- ☐ Nail clippers
- ☐ Tick tweezers
- ☐ Cat shampoo
- ☐ Brush (possibly a soft baby hair brush).
- ☐ Nopped glove
- ☐ Lotion or drops for ear cleaning
- ☐ Fluff-free cloths
- ☐ Camomile tea
- ☐ Blood-staunching stick

- Chapter 4 -

Common Disorders

For many owners, the health of their cat is at least as important as their own health, if not more so. If the animal is sick, the human also does not feel well. Luckily, we live in a time where the health system is good, even for our animals. There is plenty of medication, good vets and even clinics where our four-legged friends can be well treated.

As with humans, our cats also suffer from an assortment of disorders during their lives. Some are easy to treat, some less so. In some cases, we owners can help but in others we need to fall back on our vet or even an animal clinic.

In this chapter, I will give you a short summary about the most common disorders from which your Sphynx can suffer, caused by parasites, and about the most common gastro-intestinal sicknesses. You will get tips on how to recognise them and how best to deal with them. At this point it is important for me to stress that you should contact your vet if the problems are severe. All the tips I will give you here are meant for the less severe forms of disorder.

I will also give you some helpful information about fevers, vaccinations and castrating your Sphynx, as well as disorders typical for its breed.

The chapter will close with two check lists on how you can tell if your cat is living a healthy life and what you should keep in your cat first-aid kit.

INFESTATION OF PARASITES

Many owners of outdoor cats fear an infestation of parasites, and not without reason. These tiny insects can cause a lot of damage to our freedom-loving friends and can also be passed on to humans.

In this book I will tell you more about the three most common parasites – mites, ticks and fleas. You will hear how the insects approach their prey, what damage they can cause and what you can do about it. Sphynx cats, which are kept purely as indoor cats, seldom get parasites. However, it is also possible for cats to become infested, if they have access to a safe garden.

With all parasites, it is important to catch them early, in order to restrict the number of problems they may cause. If they are not caught early enough and your cat already has a serious infestation, it can be very difficult and time-consuming to get rid of them.

You can best detect them at an early stage, when you stick to the care and examination tips which I gave you in the previous chapter. If you examine your cat's fur regularly, and particularly after it has had an extensive romp on the fields, you are more likely to detect the parasites early and will have achieved your most important goal.

In addition, there are a few things you can do to avoid your cat from getting them in the first place and I will tell you about those in the subchapters which follow.

MITES

Mites belong to the spider family, but due to their size are often only recognisable under a microscope. There are three different subspecies which differ by their mouth tools.

Chewing mites (also known as ear mites) are at home in the ear passages of your cat and mainly feed on skin flakes. They cause skin infections and itchiness. Scratching, in turn, causes increased irritation which can lead to secondary infections and wounds.

Sucking mites (also known as dermanyssid mites) have a trunk-like mouth with which they can suck blood and the lymphatic liquids of their host. This causes the danger of pathogens transferring to the host.

The last type is the *digging mite* (also known as Sarcoptes Scabei). These "dig" through the outer skin layer, causing strong irritation which may lead to your cat injuring himself. In cats we speak of "mange", in humans we say "scabies".

Probably the biggest danger facing your Sphynx is the so-called grass mite, which belongs to the blood-sucking mite group. As the name suggests, these mites lurk in the grass, waiting for passing hosts.

Grass mites are only 0.3 millimetres in size and can be seen well because of their orange-coloured bodies. If you notice these creatures in your lawn at home, you can put out a white or light cloth on your grass during the summer. After a very short while, there will be a lot of orange spots collecting on the cloth to take a sunbathe.

They mostly attack places where they come directly in contact with your cat, such as the paws (often between the pads), the head (mostly on the bridge of the nose), the ears, the belly and the chest. They try to break into small cracks in the thinner parts of the skin and inject their saliva.

It is that saliva which causes intense irritation and, in some cases, a so-called mite allergy. The grass mites are not interested in your cat's blood but in their lymphatic fluid. You can see the affected areas because there is an orange discolouration of the skin. In addition, if you go through your cat's coat with a flea comb, you would probably notice small red spots in the fur. If not, then tap the comb onto a white cloth, where they will be more visible.

Unfortunately, there is no reliable preventative treatment against an attack of mites. There are some combi-treatments which are supposed to work against fleas, ticks and mites, but their success is dubious and questioned by many experts.

However, you are not completely helpless against them. There are a few things which you can do:

- Inspect your grass at home. If you can see grass mites, mow your lawn with greater frequency and treat it with stinging nettle compound. This successfully kills the larvae. It is important that you do not leave the cut grass on the lawn but remove it quickly.
- Examine your cat regularly after it has been playing in the meadows. The sooner you notice mite infestation, the better. If you do notice something, comb your cat thoroughly with a flea comb and give it a full bath. I suggest using a curd soap or unscented ivory soap mixture, or in particularly acute cases, a mixture of olive oil, apple vinegar and salt water together with a mild, alcohol-based solution. Ensure that you only use lukewarm water and that you rinse your Sphynx thoroughly afterwards. Both of these suggested remedies will work against the skin irritation.
- Clean the floors of your home thoroughly, and wash all the cat blankets. Vacuum other areas where your cat may have lain, such as the sofa or cat tree.

If your cat often suffers from severe mite infestation, you should ask your vet for his advice on which suitable (chemical) product it would be best to use and perhaps stop it from going outside for a while.

TICKS

As soon as the winter has passed and it starts to get warm, that is when the ticks get busy. Ticks also belong to the sucking group of the spider family, as you have probably guessed. But contrary to grass mites, which are interested in the lymphatic liquids of their hosts, ticks are only interested in blood.

At the beginning, ticks are only as big as a pinhead and can be difficult to spot or feel. But once they have found a host, and have nourished themselves on its blood for several days, the females in particular can grow up to 12 mm in size.

Ticks are mostly found on the edges of forests, in clearings, in grassland or parks. They climb on to high blades of grass or bushes and wait for their next victim. They have a particularly good sense of smell which helps them to prepare for the arrival of their host (they perceive the smell of sweat). They are also acutely aware of vibrations and changes in the CO2 content of the air. Once the tick has sensed a victim, it falls onto them and searches for a suitable place. Suitable places are mostly thin-skinned but well-circulating with blood, such as the head, haunches, ears or belly.

Most ticks prefer a particular kind of host. This is because they have usually specialised themselves on a particular host type by assimilating the anaesthetic part of their saliva secretion to them.

Did you know ...

... that there are about 900 tick species known world-wide?

About 20 of them can be found in Germany. Your cat will probably only be attacked by one of four types: The wood tick, the meadow tick, the sheep tick and the brown dog tick.

The fear that many people have for the tick is justified, as there are no other parasites which can transmit as many diseases. Ticks transmit bacteria in their saliva which can, for example, cause Borrelioses and other viruses which fall into the category of early-summer meningoencephalitis (ESME). It can also carry other parasites such as the Babesiosis which transmit toxins.

Not all such diseases are fatal but they can severely affect the health of your cat. For this reason, it is important to try and prevent your cat from getting tick bites and if your cat does get one, to recognise it quickly and remove it safely.

But what happens exactly when a tick bites?

Once it has found a suitable place, it cuts a slit in the skin of your cat with its mouthpiece and sticks its proboscis into the wound. Then it sucks the blood of its victim and at the same time introduces an anaesthetic into the wound, so that the cat does not notice that it is being bitten. The secretion also acts as an anti-inflammatory agent which blocks the immune system of the host, thereby preventing the wound from closing and enabling the blood flow to continue. During its meal, the tick excretes the undigested blood through its bowel into the wound of its host, which is what causes the previously mentioned transfer of pathogens.

Unfortunately, there are no vaccinations which work against some of these diseases, so you just need to prevent them as best you can, using the measures which are available to you. One of the most proven remedies is the spot-on preparation, which you can drizzle onto your cat's neck. This remedy lasts for about four months on average. The disadvantage, though, is that your cat is subjected to the whole toxic effect of the preparation at once. If your cat proves to be intolerant towards it or if it causes side-effects, there is little you can do about it.

One alternative is the tick collar. If you use such a collar, it is necessary to choose one which can fall off in an emergency, so that your beloved pet does not strangle itself if it gets stuck on a branch for example. The best-known collars are those with the active ingredients Deltamethrin or Amitraz. Both collars are neurotoxic for the ticks and work by continually emitting the active substance through the fat layer of the skin. It takes about a week to get the full benefit but it lasts for between four and six months.

The main advantage of these collars is that the toxic effect is released slowly into your cat and is therefore gentler on its body. If your cat is intolerant to the ingredients or the collar causes side effects, you can remove it immediately.

Both solutions involve using nerve agents so you must decide for yourself if you want to give your cat any of these toxins. In addition, when you stroke your cat, you will also come into contact with these toxins to a lesser extent. Therefore, you need to be careful with their use because some of them can be very poisonous for your feline pet. Never use products which were designed for dogs. Read the instructions on the packet carefully and make sure that the product was developed for use on cats.

The very popular amber collar is harmless for both your cat and the ticks. It is not scientifically proven that it works. Another often praised household remedy is garlic, with which you should rub your cat. This, as well as other remedies such as essential oils, lavender and lemons have not proven to be particularly effective. There is a promising natural remedy which is made from the leaves of the lemon eucalyptus. This can be bought as a collar or spot-on product. However, tests are only in the early stages. This product is said to work for only four weeks, so it needs to be applied more often.

If your cat should get bitten by a tick, despite all your efforts, it is important to remove the tick immediately. It does not matter whether you use a tick tweezer, card, lasso or normal household tweezers. Use the tool with which you feel most comfortable as all of them work equally well.

I personally prefer the tick tweezers and I will describe below how best to get rid of ticks with them.

- Firstly, make a space around the tick by pushing the fur around the area to the side.
- Place the tweezers (or whatever you are using) as close to the skin as possible and surround the tick.
- Pull the tick out quickly, but whatever you do, do not pull it out with a jerk. Ticks do not have a screw thread, so there is no need to twist it while pulling it out.
- The best result is when you are able to remove its biting apparatus intact. If not, there is no need to panic. Do not try to remove it another way as you could cause more harm than good. Leave it in, after a while it will fall out by itself.

- Destroy the tick by burning, squashing (I recommend doing that outside the house and between tissues) or dissolving it in alcohol. You should never put it into your household rubbish alive or flush it down the toilet, as ticks are very hardy little insects.
- **No-Go:** Never use other aids, such as nail polish remover, alcohol, oil, fire or glue. If you pour any of those onto the tick, it will become unnecessarily stressed, which could cause it to vomit into the wound and release even more pathogens into your cat's blood stream. In addition, you could injure your cat, particularly if you use fire!

Finally, I want to emphasise that the best agent against sicknesses caused by tick bites is regular inspection of the fur. There are no preparations presently on the market that I could recommend, as all of them have side effects or they have not been proven effective. The earlier you discover the tick, the less time it has to introduce pathogens into your cat's body. Not every tick bite causes sickness. Only 0.1 – 5% of ticks carry the ESME-Virus within them.

But what can you do if your cat gets sick? If your Sphynx starts to show symptoms after a tick bite, such as fever, fatigue or vomiting, you should contact your vet immediately. These symptoms could appear up to three weeks after the bite as the incubation period can last that long. Only your vet can confirm whether or not it is a sickness which has come from a tick bite. Make a note of when you noticed and when you removed the tick, so that your vet is given the most accurate information. I usually also take a photo of it, so that the vet can see which kind of tick it was and is able to exclude a few sicknesses from the outset.

You should also check if the bite has healed properly, over the next few weeks, and has not caused an infection. In most cases, I can say that such bites heal without problems or consequences. Make sure that you do not panic. Stay calm and be careful while removing the tick.

FLEAS

Fleas also belong to the insect family and are true survivors. Their natural habitat is meadows and bushes, but they like to live in homes too and can live there all year round. Just like ticks and mites, the fleas wait for hosts and then jump onto them as they pass by. Even though they are only 3 millimetres long, they can jump up to a height of 25 centimetres and a length of 1 metre – a great distance for such a small creature.

There are thousands of different types of fleas in the world, but the German pet cat is mostly sought by only one particular type: the cat flea, whose favourite hosts are, as the name suggests, cats. However, if no cats happen to be available, they are quite happy to attach themselves to humans. Contrary to popular belief, flea infestation has nothing to do with bad hygiene. Most pet cats become infected through contact with other cats or wild animals, such as hedgehogs, and bring them home, where they usually breed rapidly.

Did you know, ...

... that a female flea usually starts to lay eggs directly after its first blood meal?

And she lays up to 50 of them a day! The eggs fall out of the cat's fur and lie on the grass, carpet or other household textiles until they hatch about a week later. The larvae crawl into small cracks and after about 10 days are ready to find themselves a new host. In that time, a single flea could have laid up to about 850 more eggs.

The most important thing about flea infestation is that you need to catch it early so that you do not have a real invasion of fleas in the house. But how do you recognise a flea infestation?

The first sign is, of course, when you see your cat scratching itself more than usual, as the flea's saliva causes a strong itch. Some cats start to bite themselves, which often causes injury. Not all cats scratch themselves enough for you to notice. There may be very little itchiness if it is only a light infestation, but in the meantime, masses of eggs will be falling onto the carpet, the sofa, your cushions and many other places in your home.

I have taken to checking for fleas during my daily fur examination. If I see small black-brown spots, I squeeze them carefully. If they turn rust brown to red, then it is likely to be flea excrement (digested blood). If the spots do not turn reddish, it is probably just normal dirt.

I do this test on a few different places and that way I can get a good picture of whether or not my cats have fleas. If your test indicates that your cat has an infestation, you need to act quickly as it can be said that only 5% of the fleas are actually on your cat. The other 95% are to be found as fleas, larvae or eggs in the surrounding area. For this reason, it is essential that the whole region around your cat is treated. Larvae can survive up to 6 months in a sofa crevice without food, just waiting to jump onto a host again.

In case of an infestation, you should never rely solely on collars or spot-on products, which are meant for prevention purposes. They will only serve to ensure that the fleas want to escape from your cat and find a safer place to wait until the coast is clear. In the worst case, they could decide to choose you as a substitute host.

I do not need to tell you that this is not a good situation. But how can you combat flea infestation successfully? I suggest following these three steps:

1. **Kill the fleas on your Sphynx**

   Contact your vet immediately and ask him which agent is best to fight the infestation. On the one hand you need an insecticide (mostly in the form of a shampoo, spray or powder), which kills the fleas. As this agent alone will not kill all the fleas, you also need an inhibitor to prevent their development. To ensure that both compounds work at optimum levels you will need to repeat the process at certain intervals. You should discuss with your vet exactly what dosage your cat needs, and at what intervals it should be used, as these preparations are poisonous. If necessary, you should also treat other animals who live in the household with you. Be aware that some tick and flea preparations can be fatal to your cat. Your vet will know exactly what is needed and will give you the right advice.

2. **Eliminate the flea brood in the area**

   Once you have treated the fleas on your cat, you should start attacking the fleas, eggs and larvae in the area which your cat frequents. Wash all floors daily (including the corners) with a wet mop and vacuum all carpets, upholstery and other furniture. Get rid of the dust bag immediately. You can smother it with anti-flea powder if you wish. Wash all cat blankets, throws, cushions and covers at a temperature of least at 60°C. You can use a chemical cleaner in addition to that (for example on sofa covers or carpets). Remember to clean your cat's stuffed animals too. Wash all textiles at a minimum of 60°C. Treat all surfaces where your cat lies and spray its blankets etc. with a special anti-flea powder or an area spray.

Please take your vet's advice about which preparation to use and find out about the possibility of using a so-called fogger, which is a room spray which can kill fleas, eggs and larvae. Remember to clean garages, cupboards, cars thoroughly and any other places where your cat may have recently been. Even though it may seem difficult, if not impossible, you will need to keep this up for at least three months so that you can be sure you have caught all the eggs and larvae. If not, you have already pre-programmed the next flea infestation.

3. **Take preventive action**

In addition to dealing with the fleas I would also recommend using a special anti-parasitic formula to ensure that you have not done all that extra work fighting the fleas, at a not insignificant cost, only to have them return. Ask your vet which remedy is most suitable for your cat. I personally prefer repelling anti-parasitic agents which prevent the flea from biting in the first place. However, as this is a poisonous pesticide, you should check with your vet that it will work quickly but gently on your Sphynx.

In all the years I have been living together with cats I have never had a flea infestation and I am very grateful for that. However, I know, from those who have been through it, how exhausting it can be for both humans and animals. Everyone I have spoken to who has suffered from a recurrence of the infestation, said that they did not adhere 100% to the recommended measures. I can only advise: If you happen to get fleas into the house, grit your teeth and hold out for the full three months, otherwise you will end up having the same problem again within a very short time!

GASTRO-INTESTINAL DISORDERS

Just like we humans, your cat can suffer from gastro-intestinal disorders. In this chapter I will describe the four most common gastro-intestinal problems which can be found in Sphynx cats.

Some owners are not always aware that they put their cat into a danger which is quite avoidable, and I would like to change that. Sometimes it is the small things which you can do which can ensure that your Sphynx is able to live a healthier life.

I will explain exactly what those things are on the following pages.

DIARRHOEA

Diarrhoea in cats, much as in humans, is when there is an increased frequency of bowel movement where the stool consistency is mostly soft to runny. Your cat can lose as much as a litre of stool per day.

In fact, diarrhoea is one of the most common disorders in cats. The reasons for this are numerous and can range from a simple upset stomach to a serious illness. It is important for you to know that you do not need to consult your vet each time your cat has diarrhoea, nor does your cat always need medication. The general condition of your cat is key here. Keep a close watch on your Sphynx. If the symptoms last for a longer period of time or seem particularly bad to you, it is definitely advisable to consult a vet. In both of those cases, your cat could lose a lot of liquid and electrolytes, which can be dangerous.

There are several reasons why your cat can get diarrhoea. It is my experience that one (or more) of the six following situations may have caused it:

1. **Food:** In this case, your Sphynx might have been given the wrong type of food, it was eating too quickly, changes to the diet were carried out wrongly or too quickly, or your cat has an intolerance to the food it has been given. Have you recently made changes to your

cat's food? Sometimes, the proteins, carbo-hydrates or additives in the new food can cause the diarrhoea.

2. **Parasites:** Outside cats sometimes catch parasites, which can lead to diarrhoea. I will go into that in more detail in the next chapter.

3. **Viruses and Bacteria:** Just like humans, cats can also get digestive problems, which are caused by viruses or bacteria. I have noticed that younger animals suffer more frequently from this.

4. **Organ Dysfunction:** Chronic diarrhoea often occurs as a result of an organ dysfunction (such as an overactive thyroid or pancreatitis). If your cat shows symptoms such as vomiting or significant weight loss, in addition to the diarrhoea, it could be a sign of that.

5. **Poisoning:** Unfortunately, cats are not able to digest many plants and foods which humans have no problems with. Detergents or medicines, meant for humans, can also be a great danger for cats.

6. **Stress:** Many cats are very susceptible to stress and that too tends to upset their stomachs. Have you recently moved house, has a new

person come to live with you, have you recently moved your furniture around, or has another change happened in your cat's life which could cause stress?

If you are not sure whether your cat is suffering with diarrhoea, I have put together some of the most common symptoms to watch for:

- The stools are pulpy or watery.
- The stools are slimy.
- Your cat is trying but nothing is coming out.
- Your cat is going more often than usual.
- Your cat has lost weight.
- Your cat is drinking more water than usual.
- Your cat is tired and listless.

If you recognise one or more of these symptoms in your cat, it is probably suffering from diarrhoea. But how should you deal with it as the cat's owner? Should you still feed your cat or is it better to let it fast? Experts disagree on this point. For a long time, there was an unwritten rule that cats should not be fed for about 24 hours if they have diarrhoea, so that their gastro-intestinal tract can settle. Newer studies suggest that normal bowel movements can only resume when the cat is fed small amounts of light food. I, personally, have always fed my cats light food if they had diarrhoea as many cats have a good idea what is good for their bodies and what is not. As light food I would suggest boiled chicken or turkey with mashed potato or rice. Neither of these should be seasoned, of course, and you should never give your cat milk products as they could make the situation worse. Make sure that your Sphynx is drinking enough and encourage it to drink, if you need to.

One very neglected subject regarding diarrhoea is letting your cat out. Please do not let your cat out for several days (I recommend at least three days after the symptoms have gone). For one thing, you cannot keep an eye on your cat and do not know what the consistency of the stools is like or if it is behaving normally. For another, there is still the danger that your cat could infect other animals, and you want to avoid that at all costs. Even if your poor cat is crying at the door to go out, please be consistent and protect your cat as well as the others in the neighbourhood.

If the diarrhoea continues on after 24 hours, and your cat has a fever (a temperature above 39.2°C), is not eating or there is even blood in the stools, you should not hesitate to consult your vet. You need to be even more careful with kittens, or cats with prior sicknesses, than you would with a healthy cat, which otherwise appears normal.

As diarrhoea is one of the most common symptoms of a disorder, I am often asked if there are any preventive measures which can be taken. My general answer to that is: It depends. In my experience, most disorders with diarrhoea are caused by their food, so there is a lot you can do about it. Take care what you feed your cat and avoid abruptly changing food at all costs. Do not give your cat food which is meant for humans and get rid of any wet food before it goes bad. Make sure you have no poisonous plants around your home and keep detergents and medicines packed well away. If you keep to these things, you have already done a lot to avoid your cat getting sick.

You can learn how to stop your cat from getting diarrhoea which is caused by parasites in the next chapter.

WORMS

Every cat, whether it is an outdoor cat, has access to a safe garden, or is taken for walks on the lead, will get worms sooner or later – that is unavoidable. With all these activities, your cat will come into contact with the excrement of other cats and animals. They ingest the worm eggs through the nose or the mouth. It is important for you to know that you can also be infected through your cat. Stroking it, or allowing it to lick your hand could also pass on the eggs and infect you too. Pure house cats are not safe from worms either, as they can get infected through their food (mostly raw fish or meat). It is also possible that worm eggs stick to your shoes when walking and can get into the house that way too.

The following three worm types are the most common in cats:

- **Round Worms:** The larvae are often passed on through the mother's milk and develop further in the bowels. The most common symptoms are diarrhoea, weight-loss, ragged coat and hair loss.
- **Hook Worms:** The eggs of the hook worm are excreted from the cat's stools. Once outside the body, they develop into larvae and return to their hosts where they continue to develop.

Symptoms of infection are often emaciation, anaemia, and diarrhoea.

- **Tapeworms:** The Dipylidium caninum tapeworm can be injected into its host by a flea bite. Other tapeworms use a more typical prey for cats to pass on their eggs, such as birds and mice. Depending on the type, an adult tapeworm can grow to a length of 80 centimetres. Symptoms of infection often include loss of appetite, weight loss, ragged fur and itchiness in the anal region.

The visible symptoms of a worm infection will not be noticeable in your Sphynx for some time. You will notice the itchiness in the anal region when your cat begins to “scoot” along the ground by sliding along the carpet, as an example. It is possible that your cat will show no symptoms at all, as it is only acting as a temporary host, for example in the fox tapeworm. However, this particular species can lead to serious liver damage in humans.

If your cat becomes infested by worms, you will need to make a worm cure immediately. This is a chemical treatment that you can only get from your vet as it is only available on prescription. The number of repetitions you need to give depends on the compound, the severity of the infestation and the weight of your cat. For this reason, you should follow exactly the directions of your vet.

Today's worm cures are fortunately a lot less strenuous than they were a few years ago. Most cats are almost free of recognisable side-effects. However, your cat will certainly suffer from some changes to its bowel flora through the strong medicine.

Unfortunately, there is no prophylaxis or vaccine against worm infestation at present. This means that a cat can have another bout of worms as soon as 24 hours after finishing the worm treatment.

For this reason, many vets suggest using de-worming treatments regularly – every three to four months – so that the parasites have no chance of survival, even if there are no apparent symptoms.

However, this recommendation is not without its critics as the pharmaceutical companies have not yet carried out any long-term studies about the regular use of their treatments. It is not yet clear how the continual use of their compounds will affect your cat.

If you want to avoid giving your cat worm tablets its whole life, but at the same time be sure that it has not become infected, there is one other effective alternative: A faeces analysis.

For this you have to collect stool samples from your cat on three consecutive days. A single sample would probably not be enough as you cannot see the worm eggs in every stool.

Send the samples to a veterinary medicine laboratory or to your vet and have them analysed for parasites. If the results are positive, there is no alternative but to administer another dose of the cure. If the results are negative, you can rest assured and if you wish you can repeat the analysis every three to four months.

This involves a significant amount of effort on the part of the cat owner, but the method is much less strenuous for your cat. An analysis costs between 15 and 30 Euros and has the advantage that your cat does not need to undergo unnecessary medical treatment.

Decide for yourself which method you prefer. You can either treat your cat when it shows acute symptoms, or you give it regular prophylactic treatments, or as a third alternative you can have its stools regularly examined for parasites. My personal recommendation is that you consider variations 2 or 3. If your Sphynx is a pure housecat, it is enough to have it examined once per year.

POISONS AND OTHER PROBLEMATIC SUBSTANCES

Did you know that many foodstuffs which we humans can eat without problems can be dangerous, if not fatal, for your Sphynx?

You should never feed your cat any of the following foodstuffs, as they could be life-threatening for it:

- **Avocado**: The ingredient Persian can lead to serious heart muscle inflammation in your cat which could be fatal.
- **Onions, garlic, leek, chives**: The sulphur contained in these foods can destroy the red corpuscles in your cat's blood, so never give it your food leftovers. It does not matter if they are raw, cooked or dried. You should always keep spice plants away from your cat.
- **Chocolate and cocoa:** Cocoa (including chocolate) contains theobromine and theophylline, which are poisonous for cats. The darker the chocolate, the greater the proportion of cocoa and therefore the more poisonous the chocolate becomes. The result could be cardiac arrhythmia, muscle tremor and seizures.

- **Grapes and Raisins**: Grapes and raisins contain oxalic acid which can lead to a fatal kidney failure.
- **Raw pork**: The Aujeszky's Disease virus, which can be found in raw pork, is incurable for cats and is always fatal.
- **Alcohol**: Self-evidently, alcohol can lead to your cat suffering from liver and kidney failure.
- **Caffeine**: Caffeine contains Methylxanthines which can be fatal to the nervous system of your cat. Coffee and tea are therefore taboo.

The following foodstuffs are not usually fatal but are poisonous for your four-legged friend and could lead to serious problems:

- **Bacon**: Particularly fatty foods, such as bacon or poultry skin cause metabolic disorders which can cause problems with the kidneys or pancreas.
- **Poultry bones**: Cats should never be given poultry bones, no matter whether cooked or raw. The thin bones split quickly and can get stuck in their throats.
- **Raw beans**: The toxin Phasin inhibits protein synthesis and can cause the red corpuscles to

stick together. If you are going to feed your cat beans, ensure that you cook them first.

- **Raw solanaceous plants**: Raw potatoes, tomatoes and aubergines should never be given to your cat. They can cause diarrhoea, vomiting and brain disorders. The most dangerous part of the plant is the skin. However, these vegetables are no longer a problem once they are cooked.
- **Milk**: As many cats have a lactose intolerance, you should not give them any milk which contains lactose.
- **Salt**: Giving salt to your cat can cause it to develop kidney problems.

This was a summary of the main and most dangerous substances for your cat. If you notice that your Sphynx is not able to cope with other foods, you should discontinue feeding them.

There are also a variety of house plants which can be dangerous for cats. Below are some of the more common:

- Aloe Vera
- Cyclamen
- Amaryllis
- Azalea or Rhododendron

- Philodendron
- Caladium
- Cala
- Chili
- Chrysanthemum
- Ivy
- Aureus
- Spathiphyllum
- Kalanchoe
- Lily
- Mistletoe
- Narcissus
- Palm fern (Cycas Revoluta)
- Aralia (Schefflera)
- Tulip
- Poinsettia
- Castor Oil Plant (Ricinus)

For the sake of your Sphynx, you should ban all these plants out of your living areas. As my list is by no means exhaustive, I suggest checking each new house plant arriving in your house for its suitability. A quick check in the internet should be enough to find out if the plant is poisonous for your cat or not.

CANCERS

Current studies show that one in every two cats will suffer from a tumour at some time in its life. This makes cancer undisputedly the most common cause of death in cats.

It is not exactly clear what causes this, whether it be the consequences of living with humans, increased life expectancy, over-breeding or simply the improved and more intensive veterinary medicine available.

Happily, there are also many therapies which can significantly extend the life expectancy of such cats. Tumours can be surgically removed and their growth can be inhibited by radiation or chemo therapies. Radio and immune therapies are also among today's remedies which may increase the life expectancy of your Sphynx, or even cure it.

Cat owners should always weigh the benefits of increasing the length of their cat's life against the quality of its life. Extending its life through surgery or medicines, even if the quality of its life is badly impaired, may help the owner but does not always help the pet. Even if it is difficult, an owner has to be able to make the right choice for the animal.

The best care is better than any therapy, but there are varying opinions about what that should look like. Vets have not been able to establish a link between castration and a reduction in cancer. Castrated animals become just as ill as their "intact" cousins. The only link that vets have been able to establish is that older cats are more prone to cancer than young ones.

Correct nutrition has also been linked to cancer care. However, this has not been scientifically proven. For this reason, I cannot offer you any recommendations on the best care for your cat in this respect. That said, I can give you a few tips as to how you can recognise cancer early. Early detection is very important as tumours spread quickly in cats and therefore every minute counts in improving the chances of curing your pet.

Below you will find the most common signs that your Sphynx could have a tumour:

- **Lumps on or under the skin:** When stroking your cat, be aware of any hardening, lumps or bumps on or under the skin of your Sphynx. These can be found anywhere on the body.

- **Loss of appetite and unusual loss of weight:** Loss of appetite does not necessarily mean that there is a tumour. However, if it continues over a period of time, you need to have your cat examined. If your cat suddenly loses weight without changing its eating habits, there is definitely a reason to become concerned, as a malignant tumour would change the metabolism of your Sphynx.

- **Frequent diarrhoea, blood in the vomit or blood in the diarrhoea:** If you see any of these symptoms you should contact your vet. The same applies if your Sphynx has trouble urinating or defecating.
- **Lethargy or noticeable loss of stamina:** Many owners believe that these symptoms are part of growing old. This is also true, but if the symptoms come suddenly and strongly, you should take notice.
- **Changes in behaviour:** If your Sphynx suddenly becomes withdrawn or is suddenly particularly clingy, this could also be a symptom.

All these symptoms could be, but are not necessarily, hints that your Sphynx has cancer. It would not do any harm to have them checked anyway by your vet. Do not panic as these symptoms can also apply to much less serious disorders, such as a parasite infection.

FEVER

The borderline to a fever for cats is not as exact as with us humans. A healthy Sphynx can have an optimum temperature of between 38° and 39° C.

I would suggest taking your cat's temperature several times while it is healthy, so that you can tell if it is becoming sick. Make sure that your cat is lying quietly, as stress or physical exertion can raise the temperature for a short time. We speak generally of a "light fever" if the temperature is higher than 39°C, but here there is no need to worry. As I mentioned previously, this could be due to stress or physical exertion. If its temperature rises above 40°C, you can usually feel the heat coming off your cat. It may start to show outward signs of becoming unwell, such as loss of appetite or general lethargy.

You should contact your vet if its temperature exceeds 41°C. It could be dangerous for your Sphynx to have a fever that high for too long.

If its temperature exceeds 42°C this could be very dangerous as the body's own proteins start to clump together – a process which cannot be reversed. At the latest, you should now be contacting your vet or even a pet clinic.

Having a fever does not have to be a bad thing. It is the way that the body destroys pathogens. In addition, it shows that your cat's immune system is working. Fever reduction medicines should not be used unless the fever becomes very high or remains for a long time. Again, never use medicines which are meant for humans, they can be fatal for animals.

How do you measure the temperature on your cat?

The simplest way is with a normal thermometer. I bought one especially for my cats so that we humans do not have to use the same one. I use a disposable cover to reduce the amount of cleaning necessary afterwards. The best kind of thermometer to buy is one with a flexible tip, they are more comfortable for your cat and can reduce the danger of injury at the same time.

Dampen the thermometer slightly before use and ensure that it is not too cold. Hold your Sphynx's tail firmly at the base and lift it slightly. Insert the thermometer carefully and wait for the signal before you remove it and check the temperature.

It is best to practise this procedure from kitten age onwards and praise your cat lavishly for standing still. Follow the procedures which you use for other health screening examinations. If you have a particularly nervous or shy cat, you will probably have difficulties using a normal thermometer. If this is the case, you could use an infra-red thermometer and measure your cat's temperature in its ear. This makes the process much easier and less complicated. However, the measurement taken by an infra-red thermometer in the ear is significantly less accurate. My first choice will always be a classical thermometer if you are dealing with a well-trained cat.

If you do not have a thermometer handy, you can recognise if your cat has a fever by observing the following symptoms:

- The insides of your cat's ears feel warmer than usual, even hot.
- You notice that your cat is drinking much more than usual even though it is not very hot, or it stops drinking altogether.
- When stroking your cat, it feels warmer than usual, particularly around the nose.
- Your cat generally looks exhausted without having had much physical exertion.

If you see any of the above symptoms, you can assume that your Sphynx has a fever. Watch your cat carefully. If you have the feeling that the situation is getting worse or has been going on for too long, you should contact your vet.

VACCINATIONS

The vaccination of cats causes as intense a discussion and disagreement as it does with human vaccinations. However, in contrast to humans, there is no general compulsory vaccination programme, so it is up to each owner to decide whether to have his cat vaccinated or not.

Of course, every owner wants the best for his cat, but there is a great divide in opinions as to how this can be achieved. A vaccination, depending on the active ingredient, can have a good to very good protection against bacteria as well as viral diseases. They do not only protect animals from catching such diseases but can also even help to eradicate or at least to repress them. If a pathogen cannot find a host over an extended period of time, the population of this pathogen reduces automatically.

The Standing Committee of Veterinary Medicine's Immunisation Committee (known in Germany as the StIKoVet) regularly issues recommendations regarding vaccinations in two forms: Core and non-core vaccinations. Core vaccinations are (according to the StIKoVet) essential vaccinations which are important because a disease has become prevalent for which there are few or no treatments. Non-core vaccinations are optional and depend on such things as the health of the animal or any previous illnesses the animal may have had.

Core vaccinations include.

- Feline Panleukopenia
- Cat flu

The following vaccinations are less essential and are considered to be non-core.

- Feline Leukaemia (recommended for outdoor cats up to the age of 7 years)
- Rabies (recommended for outdoor cats)
- Feline infectious Peritonitis (only when certain medical indicators are present)

If you are wondering if you should have your indoor cat vaccinated, I can recommend it thoroughly. Even though indoor cats only have a controlled contact to other cats and animals, there are typical sicknesses which can be spread without direct contact, such as Panleukopenia and cat flu. For this reason, the core vaccinations for these two sicknesses are essential, in my opinion, for both indoor and outdoor cats.

If you decide to have your cat vaccinated, it is important that it gets the primary as well as the subsequent booster injections. The primary vaccination will build up immunity to particular pathogens in your cat's body. The booster injections will ensure continuous protection.

Only healthy cats should be immunised. Cats which are sick, cats with weakened immune systems or which have parasites should not be vaccinated. Many experts also discourage immunising cats which are too old. Your cat should always be fully examined before vaccinations are given, including having a blood test.

You should ensure that your kitten receives its primary vaccinations at between 8 and 15 months. The procedure and costs can be determined in consultation with your vet. You should also discuss the appointments for its booster injections early and perhaps arrange for your vet to send you a reminder.

Did you know, ...

... that rabies has been completely eradicated in Germany since 2008?

This means that, if you live in Germany, you will not have to immunise your Sphynx against Rabies. However, if you live in, or travel to any other parts of Europe (or the world), vaccination quickly becomes imperative. If your Sphynx has bitten another animal, or even a human, it is important that you can present a valid rabies vaccination certificate. Failure to do so could result in your cat having to be put to sleep.

PANLEUKOPENIA UND CAT FLU

As you know from the previous chapter, both indoor and outdoor cats can catch Panleukopenia and cat flu. As both illnesses are unfortunately so common, I will go into much more detail about them in this chapter.

Panleukopenia sounds like a sickness which will quickly cause death and which is very infectious. Nowadays, there are good therapies for this sickness and, if treated early enough, should not lead to death. The sickness is caused by the feline Panleukopenia virus. The danger in this virus lies in its longevity and resistance. At room temperature, it can live up to a year on objects, such as toys, clothes or baskets, and does not respond to disinfectants. This means that re-infection can happen at any time and transmission of the virus can occur, even in indoor cats.

After an incubation period of two to six days, you will usually notice the following symptoms on your Sphynx:

- It looks drained and tired.
- It loses its appetite.
- It suffers from bouts of fever. The temperature can climb up to 41°C, sink, only to rise shortly afterwards again.
- She vomits.

Unfortunately, all these signals are not specific to Panleukopenia and can be due to a number of other sicknesses. It can also run a peracute course. That means that your cat shows none of the above symptoms but suddenly becomes very ill and dies of the shock. This virus always attacks the intestines, bones and lymphatic vessels. Infected animals later begin to suffer from bloody diarrhoea, which can discharge vast amounts of the virus, leading to further dissemination of the virus. It also produces a shortage in the number of white blood cells in the blood, which will cause a massive weakness in the immune system.

In most cases, the virus affects young cats up to about two years of age, as their immune system is not yet fully developed. Fully-grown cats can also get the virus, although it is less common. A visit to your vet is essential. Within a few hours, this virus can lead to the death of a kitten. However, if it is treated in time, the chances of recovery are very good. Having said that, the mortality rate lies between 25 – 75%. The big fluctuation is due to the differences in the health of the cats who suffer from the virus, and which virus strain is involved. After the sickness is over, your Sphynx will be infectious to other cats for a long time and you should avoid giving it access to unvaccinated cats. Luckily, the virus is not dangerous for humans.

In comparison, cat flu is far less harmful – but do not be deceived by its name. Cat flu refers to a sickness of the respiratory tract, mucus membranes and the head area of the cat, which can be caused by various viruses and bacteria. Cats can catch it from each other or, similarly to Panleukopenia, from objects. It is important for you to know that, unlike Panleukopenia, the bacterial pathogens of cat flu can be dangerous for humans!

After an incubation period of about five days, you will probably notice the following symptoms:

- Lethargy, exhaustion
- Fever
- Loss of appetite
- Coughing and snorting
- Purulent discharge (pus) through the eyes and nose

Once the animal has been affected by the virus, the vet will prescribe a broad-spectrum antibiotic and an anti-viral and immune-system-strengthening agent. In order to find the exact medication your cat needs, your vet must take blood and swabs. The treatment is time-consuming and usually very expensive. The earlier the sickness is detected, the greater the chances are that your beloved pet will recover.

Valid for both sicknesses: The best protection is the prevention through immunisation. I want to stress the importance of it and ask you to contact your vet if you are unsure.

CASTRATION

The cat is Germany's favourite pet. According to a public survey carried out in 2019, there were about 15 million cats in German households at that time. The German Association of Veterinary Surgeons believed that there were 8 million house cats, living more or less wild on the streets during the same period. This was a number which was shocking and created quite a few problems. In Germany, there is no federal obligatory castration for cats, even though an increasing number of cities and communities create their own laws for it. You need to find out if your area has such a regulation. On the Association's internet page, you will be able to find a summary which will help you.

Since cats like your Sphynx become sexually mature at the age of seven months, outdoor cats in particular can usually reproduce uncontrollably. The unwanted kittens are killed, more often than not, or abandoned or put into animal shelters. These are already bursting at the seams and it is not a secret that there is not enough space for new cats. Apart from avoiding unchecked reproduction, castration can offer other advantages for your cat:

- Castrated cats live longer. The reasons for that are that castrated cats are less likely to be infected during territorial fights or fights with competitors or during mating. Among those infections are immunodeficiency diseases, such as cat AIDS or feline leukaemia, which almost always end in death.

- No heat in cats and no marking behaviour in cats.
- Hormone disorders are minimised.
- The cats become more affectionate, less likely to stray and are therefore less likely to become victims of vehicle accidents.

Of course, it is up to you whether you want your cat to be castrated. However, it is important that you think carefully about the subject, considering the pros and cons and what actually happens during castration. You need to have all the information at your disposal, before you can make a decision in the best interests of your cat.

When we speak of castration, we are talking about a veterinary intervention which removes the gonads of your cat. In male cats it is their testicles and by females it is the ovaries which are removed. Castration is a permanent intervention which cannot be reversed. It is carried out under full anaesthetic, which can always carry some risk and there can also be some side effects

Did you know ...

... that, in spite of popular opinion, castration and sterilisation are two completely separate types of operation and have nothing to do with the sex of the animal?

We speak of a sterilisation when only the spermatic ducts or the fallopian tube is severed. The animal is infertile but the sex drive remains intact. For this reason, male and female cats are usually castrated and not sterilised.

The right time to castrate is when the cat becomes sexually mature, that is usually between the sixth and eleventh month. There is no scientific reason for the belief that it is best to castrate cats after their first heat or even after their first litter. However, I would recommend speaking about it first with your vet. The costs will conform to the statutory fee tariff for veterinary surgeons. Depending on the severity of the procedure, vets have the choice of charging single, double or treble the tariff on the schedule. As of 14th February, 2020, the single tariff, for a male cat, amounts to 19.24 Euros and for females, the tariff is 57.72 Euros. The difference in price has its reasons. The intervention for females is considerably more complex. In addition to the above tariff, there will be costs for the examination, the anaesthesia and care of the wound.

It is important that your cat is thoroughly examined before the castration, because only healthy animals should undergo such an operation. This includes an examination for parasites. When the time comes, you must ensure that your cat does not eat anything for at least 12 hours before the procedure. You should also not feed your cat on the evening before (if this is more than 12 hours before the operation). On the day of the operation, it should not drink anything either.

I will describe two methods of castration below, so that you have an idea what happens during the procedure:

- For a male cat, the pubic area is shaved, disinfected and sterilised, ready for castration. The vet pulls the testicles forwards and opens them with a scalpel. He pulls out the testicles together with the spermatic cord and ties them up. Then he separates the testicles from the spermatic cord and removes them. Lastly, he unbinds the spermatic cord and sews up the wound.
- With a female cat the belly area is shaved, disinfected and sterilised. The scalpel cut starts just under the belly button and along the lower

abdomen. The vet then removes the ovaries. The inner wound is sewn up using absorbable sutures and the outer wound is closed with non-absorbable sutures.

After about 10 days, in both cases, you will have to return to the vet to have the outer sutures removed. The inner sutures will dissolve by themselves over time.

Directly after the operation, your cat will sleep for another hour or two. When it wakes up, it will be very groggy and will be in a lot of pain. Therefore, it is important that you give it all the painkillers which your vet has prescribed. Cats are often unable to tell us when they are in pain. They are quiet and do not move much; very few of them whine or squeak.

After the procedure has taken place, you should be prepared to give your cat less food or for it to have more exercise than before. After castration, the metabolism reduces by about 30 percent, even though your cat will have the same appetite as before. Many cats will become overweight after they have been castrated. You can ensure that this does not happen by controlling its food intake and increasing its playtimes. That has the added advantage that your cat will feel better and become more bonded to you.

It is up to you whether you want your cat to go through this. I hope to have given you some information in this chapter which can help you to make your decision.

DISEASES TYPICAL FOR YOUR BREED

Unfortunately, with your Sphynx, you have chosen a breed which relatively often suffers from immune deficiencies, other disorders or a reduced life expectancy, due to its intensive inbreeding. In addition, this breed carries an increased risk of suffering from the following (hereditary) sicknesses. I urge you to speak about this situation with your breeder and ask about any sicknesses that animals from previous litters have suffered.

The most common of these conditions are as follows:

- **Hypertrophic Cardiomyopathy:** This is a condition which specifically affects the heart muscles, which, unfortunately, is hard to detect without a veterinary test. When the first symptoms appear, such as paralysis, respiratory distress and loss of appetite, there is not much time to save the cat's life. The heart walls thicken causing difficulty for the heart to pump enough blood. There is no known cure, only a reduction in the symptoms is possible up to now. Affected animals should never be used for breeding.
- **Cysts in the Kidneys**: Polycystic kidney disease is when cysts develop in the kidneys, which

grow constantly and can eventually affect other organs. Unfortunately, there is also no cure for this sickness, although pain relief and prolongation of life is certainly possible. The symptoms are vomiting, loss of appetite, great thirst and an increase in urination volume.

- **Whisker Deformity:** Sphynx cats will not only have curly fur, but also curly whiskers, due to a gene mutation. This can lead to a massive disturbance in its sense of orientation. This is one of the reasons why this breed has been classified in Germany as "relevant for animal protection".

All these sicknesses can occur to your Sphynx, but not necessarily. To be clear, that probability is relatively low, as there are many more healthy cats than sick ones. However, it is important that I make you aware of these breed-typical disorders, which appear to happen more often to a Sphynx than with other breeds.

CHECKLIST: FOR A HEALTHY CAT LIFE

- ☐ Am I feeding my cat in a manner which is suitable for its kind?
- ☐ Does it have a normal weight?
- ☐ Does my Sphynx always have access to fresh and clean water?
- ☐ Is my Sphynx living in a clean environment (plates, sleeping place, toys, litter box, etc)?
- ☐ Am I carrying out regular examinations and do I know my cat's normal temperature? Do I conscientiously keep my appointments (for example for immunisations)?
- ☐ Am I looking after my Sphynx's fur reliably and am I checking it regularly for ticks?
- ☐ Is my Sphynx getting enough exercise? Is it able to frolic about, run and play? Am I offering enough variety in its everyday life?
- ☐ Am I challenging this clever cat enough intellectually (for example through systematic training)?

- Can I, in all honesty, say that my Sphynx is happy with me or would it be better off somewhere else?

CHECKLIST: CAT FIRST AID KIT

- ☐ Remedy for wound infections and healing ointment (I recommend iodine ointment or a multi-purpose antiseptic cream – if in doubt, call a vet).
- ☐ Bandaging suitable for a cat
- ☐ Cat shoes
- ☐ Waterproof plaster
- ☐ Compresses and bandages
- ☐ Thermometer (with disposable covers)
- ☐ Tick tweezers (or similar tool for removing ticks)
- ☐ Torch
- ☐ Blood clotting pen (optional)
- ☐ Cat muzzle
- ☐ Disposable gloves
- ☐ Tweezers

- Chapter 5 -

SPECIAL CHAPTER: HOME-COOKED CAT FOOD

It gives me a great deal of pleasure to spoil my cats a bit by preparing a home-made snack or home-cooked meal for them, from time to time.

On the following pages I will introduce you to my 10 favourite recipes with which I can spoil my cats and which they eat with great pleasure. Please remember that this type of food should remain an exception and should not substitute their whole diet. My recipes can be considered single food.

I hope you have a lot of fun following the recipes and baking!

RECIPE 1: SALMON BISCUITS

Ingredients:

- 125 ml tinned salmon, well drained
- 250 ml full corn breadcrumbs
- 60 ml Wholewheat flour
- 1 tbsp. vegetable oil
- 1 beaten egg
- ½ tsp. brewer's yeast (e.g., crushed brewer's yeast tablets)

Preparation:

1. Preheat oven to 180°C.
2. Mash the salmon into a bowl. I usually use a fork.
3. Mix the remaining ingredients into the salmon and form into a dough.
4. Roll the dough onto a floured surface and cut out the biscuits using a cutting form.
5. Bake the biscuits for 15 – 20 minutes then leave to cool.

The biscuits keep very well in an air-tight container in the fridge. Only feed a few biscuits per day.

RECIPE 2: WILD POTATO BISCUITS

Ingredients:

- 200 g potato flour
- 100g minced game[4] (alternatively, you can use beef, or poultry hearts)
- 2 eggs
- 2 tbsp rapeseed oil
- Approx. 50 ml Water

Preparation:

1. Mix all ingredients together
2. Roll the mixture into a finger-thick mass on a floured surface and cut out the biscuits into any shape you like.
3. Lay them onto a baking tray lined with greaseproof paper.
4. Bake at 160°C for about 25 minutes
5. Leave to cool, then they are ready to serve.

[4] Cut into small pieces and fed through a grinding machine

RECIPE 3: LUNG WITH RICE

Ingredients:

- 250 g beef lung (best if fresh from butcher
- 125 g round-grain rice
- 1 carrot
- 1 banana
- 1 tbsp olive oil

Preparation:

1. Cut the beef lung into small pieces and boil together with the rice for about 20 minutes in 250 ml water.
2. Cut the carrot and banana and mix in a mixer together with the olive oil
3. Mix together with the rice and lung
4. Serve all when it is sufficiently cool.

RECIPE 4: CHICKEN WITH MILLET AND EGG

Ingredients:

- 200 g chicken or turkey breast
- 1 boiled egg
- 150 g millet
- 1 - 5 lettuce leaves
- A little olive oil

Preparation:

1. Boil the chicken breast in a saucepan with water at the highest setting until it is cooked through.
2. Sear the chicken. In the meantime, place the millet with a little olive oil and water in a medium-sized saucepan and bring to the boil.
3. Let the saucepan with the millet simmer on a low heat for about 12 minutes. Allow to drain.
4. Chop the egg and lettuce leaves and add to the millet mixture.
5. Cut the cooked and cooled meat into bite-sized pieces and add to the millet and other ingredients.
6. Leave to cool before serving.

RECIPE 5: RICE AND GROUND BEEF CAKE

Ingredients:

- 150 g ground beef
- 1 egg
- 40 g carrot
- 40 g zucchini
- 50 g rice
- 1 slice wholewheat bread
- 1 slice of cut white bread

Preparation:

1. Soften the white bread in water.
2. Grate the carrot and zucchini.
3. Cut the wholewheat bread into small squares.
4. Squeeze the extra water out of the softened white bread.
5. Mix all the ingredients into a smooth mass.
6. Fill the mass into a cake form.
7. Bake the cake at 200°C for 30 minutes.
8. Leave to cool before eating.

RECIPE 6: BEEF MIX

Ingredients:

- 100 g beef gullet
- 40 g beef spleen
- 40 g green beef belly
- 60 g buckwheat
- 1 carrot
- ½ apple (cored)
- 1 tbsp rapeseed oil

Preparation:

1. Cut the gullet into cat-sized pieces and steam it at a low temperature.
2. Cut the other offal (spleen and belly) into small pieces but do not cook them.
3. Boil the buckwheat according to the instructions on the packaging.
4. Poach the carrot in a water bath then puree it.
5. Grate the apple
6. Mix all ingredients together with the oil and your healthy beef mix is ready.

RECIPE 7: WILD TURKEY (BARF)

Ingredients:

- 2 turkey gullets (best when bought fresh from your butcher)
- 40 g turkey liver
- 100 g turkey goulash
- 40 g broccoli
- 1 carrot
- 1 tbsp dried sage
- 1 tbsp rapeseed oil

Preparation:

1. Mix the meats together.
2. Lightly steam the broccoli (left raw it will cause flatulence) and chop it into small pieces.
3. Grate the carrot.
4. Mix the carrot and broccoli and puree them together.
5. Fold the sage and oil into the mixture.
6. Mix everything together with the meat.

RECIPE 8: ITALIAN TURKEY

Ingredients:

- 300 g turkey
- 60 g buckwheat pasta
- 1 carrot
- 1 cup shredded beetroot
- 1 tbsp shredded linseed
- 1 tbsp rapeseed oil

Preparation:

1. Cut the turkey into rough pieces and steam it under low heat until it is cooked.
2. Cook the pasta until soft.
3. Grate the carrot.
4. Mix all the ingredients together and allow to cool before serving.

RECIPE 9: CAT ICE CREAM WITH BANANA AND APPLE

Ingredients:

- 1 banana
- 1 apple
- 1 pack of cottage cheese
- 1 tbsp lactose-free (!) yoghurt

Preparation:

1. Puree the banana and cored (but not peeled apple).
2. Mix the puree with the cottage cheese and yoghurt.
3. Fill the mass into small containers and freeze.

When the temperature is very warm, you can give your cat a real treat. I chose those two types of fruit which my cats love to eat most, but you can exchange them with any other kind of fruit. The ice cream is meant as a snack for your cat, not a complete meal. I always feed this to my cats outside because they make such a mess.

Recipe 10: Cat ice cream with liver sausage and oat flakes

Ingredients:

- 1 piece of liver sausage
- 20 g oat flakes
- 1 packet of cottage cheese
- 1 tbsp lactose-free (!) yoghurt

Preparation:

1. Mix all the ingredients together.
2. Fill the mass into small containers and freeze.

- Chapter 6 -

CONCLUSION

You have done it! By reading the previous chapters, you have learned a lot about the nutrition and care of your Sphynx. This knowledge should not only help you to give your Sphynx the correct nutrition but will ensure that you keep a cool head should your cat get sick. In addition, you have learned how to groom and take care of your cat. You know how to examine your cat's eyes, ears, teeth, paws, fur and skin.

You know what you need to watch out for in order to recognise a parasite infestation in good time. In addition, you have learned to understand what is normal for your cat and what you need to have checked by the vet. You have obtained a well-stocked range of care products and a first-aid kit which is suitable for your Sphynx.

You have learned a lot about your cat's nutrition and know what to watch out for when buying pre-prepared foods. You know the advantages and disadvantages of alternative feeding, such as home-cooked foods as well as BARF, vegetarian or vegan foods. You know how much water your cat needs and have learned some simple tricks to motivate it to drink. The recipes you have learned will allow you to treat your cat and make it very happy. My best tip is to give it the ice-cream on very hot days – your Sphynx will be unbelievably grateful to you!

You both have my sincerest good wishes and I hope that my tips about sicknesses never have to be used! But if so, I am sure that you will now recognise them early enough.

SPACE FOR YOUR NOTES

BOOK RECOMMENDATION FOR YOU

Grab the first part now and discover how to raise your Sphynx Kitten!

RAISING A SPHYNX CAT – Guidebook how to educate a Sphynx Kitten

Educating cats is often:

» ... considered unnecessary,
» ... described as impossible and
» ... tried by very few cat owners.

What does cat training mean and what is it good for? How can you and your Sphynx profit from it, even without previous experience.

The first thing to understand is how a cat sees its world, what is “normal” for it and how that knowledge can be useful for you. In addition, the characteristics of each breed are crucial when considering training your cat. Your Sphynx, for example has different characteristics to those of a Persian Cat and you need to take that into consideration in your planning.

Satisfy your curiosity and learn background information about your cat, read reports on other experiences and obtain step-by-step instructions and insider tips which are tailor-made for your Sphynx.

Get your copy of this book today and find out ...

» ... how your Sphynx sees its world...
» ... and how you can progressively train your cat to achieve the best results.

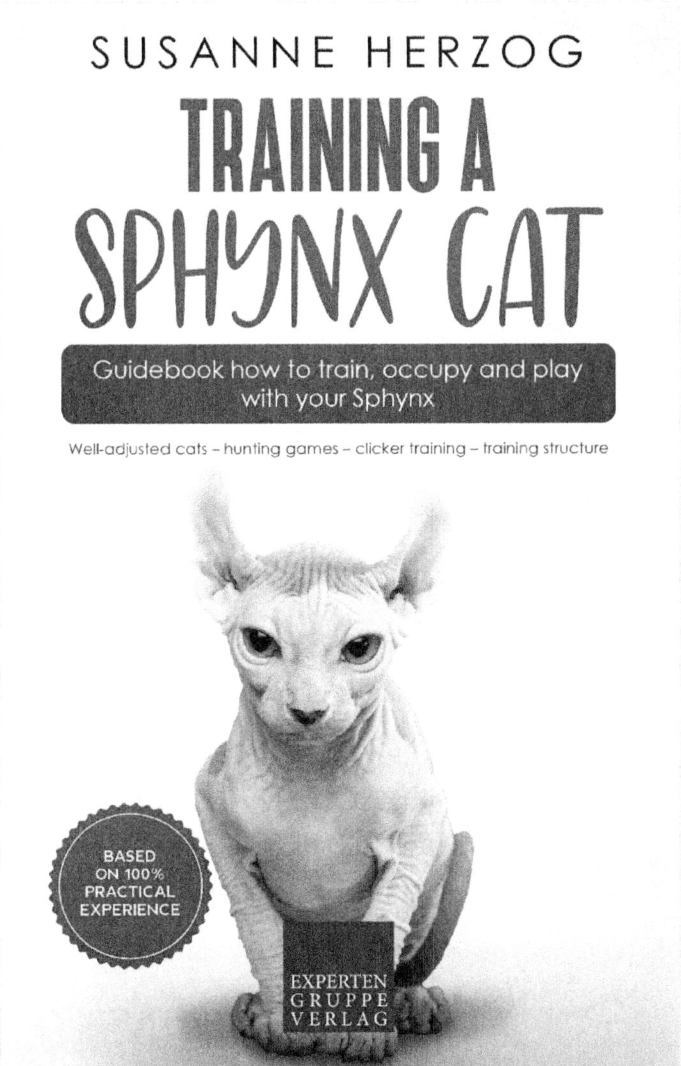

Grab the second volume now and discover how to train and occupy your Sphynx Cat!

TRAINING A SPHYNX CAT - Guidebook how to train, occupy and play with your Sphynx

Cat training is often ...

» ... confused with the classical basic education of a kitten.
» ... only thought practical for particularly talented cats.
» ... thought of as being too difficult to do without any previous experience

What difference does cat training make and what is it good for? And how can you and your Sphynx profit from it?

Does your cat sometimes seem to have too much pent-up energy and is not powered out enough, or perhaps it is bored? Then cat training is exactly the right thing for you. The simple but effective methods used in cat training will help you to tire out your Sphynx in a way which is compatible with its breed and, more importantly, have fun, while at the same time increasing the bond between you.

Satisfy your curiosity and learn background information, read reports on other experiences and obtain step-by-step instructions and insider tips which are tailor-made for your Sphynx.

Get your copy of this book today and experience...

» ... how you can build up a unique relationship with your Sphynx and
» ... how you can power out your cat physically and mentally in a manner appropriate to its species.

Get the new mandala coloring book now with 55 wonderful cat motifs!

MANDALA COLORING BOOK CATS - 55 animal motifs (cat theme) to colour-in for adults and children

Do you love colouring-in and are you very fond of cats? Perhaps you are feeling very stressed at the moment and need a moment to relax, a time to switch-off and enjoy your own company?

You can do that with this book. Inside, 55 hand-picked motifs of cats are waiting for you to bring them to life. Every picture is crafted with great care, creating a wonderful combination of animal drawing and mandalas.

While you are colouring-in, you will notice:

- how you can immerse yourself in the fantastic world of mandalas,
- how your body and mind come to rest and
- how you can leave stress behind you, through mindfulness and patience.

Immerse yourself in the world of mandalas and discover the 55 beautiful and individual cat mandalas contained in this colouring book. As if that is not enough, you will also receive additional 8 mandalas from the fantastic world of our colouring books – free!

Stimulate your imagination and enjoy a moment of peace and tranquillity, just for you!

DID YOU ENJOY MY BOOK?

Now you have read my book, you know how to care for your Sphynx correctly and how to avoid or deal with possible ailments which may affect it. For that reason, I would like to ask you a small favour. Amazon regards reviews as an important part of every product offered. It is one of the first things customers will look for and often they are a decisive factor as to whether a product will be bought or not. This factor is becoming increasingly important, taking into consideration the endless choice which Amazon provides.

If you enjoyed my book, I would be more than grateful if you could leave a review for me. How do you do that? Just click on the following button on Amazon's product page:

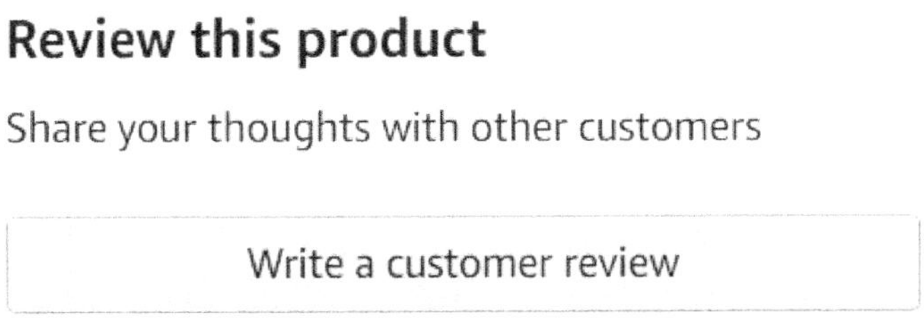

Briefly describe what you particularly liked about it or how you think I can improve this book. It only takes 2 minutes, and that is a promise! You can be sure that I will personally read every review, as it will help me to improve my book and to modify it to suit your needs.

Therefore, I say:

THANK YOU VERY MUCH!

Yours Susanne

REFERENCES

Die Haltung von Katzen, unter Beteiligung von Deutscher Tierschutzbund, 2007

Artgerechte Haltung von Katzen in der Wohnung, von del Amo, Celina erschienen in team.konkret, 01.02.2011

Katzen: Spielgefährten auf Samtpfoten ; [Tips für den Kauf ; Katzenhaltung und -pflege ; mit Katzen leben ; Lexikon der Katzenrassen], von Grau, Joachim, 1998

Hygiene und Ernährung bei der Haltung von Hunden und Katzen, von Kraft, H erschienen in Praktische Tierarzt

Krankheiten der Katze:2 Management von Haltung und Zucht, 6., aktualisierte Auflage., erschienen in Krankheiten der Katze, 2019

Katzen: unsere zärtlichen Freunde ; Anschaffung, Rassen, Abstammung, Erziehung, Pflege, Gesundheit, Zusammenleben, unter Beteiligung von Breuer, Antje, 1999

Unsauberkeit bei Katzen: Ursachen verstehen, vorbeugen und helfen, 1. Aufl., von Jones, Renate, 2013

DuMont's grosses Katzenbuch: Wesen und Verhalten, Anschaffung, Pflege und Ernährung, Krankheiten ; Zucht, Rassen, Katzenausstellungen, von Cutts, Paddy, 1993

Zur Kulturgeschichte der Hauskatze unter besonderer Berücksichtigung ihrer Erkrankungen, von Jores, Nicola Lesley, 2004

Verhaltensstörungen bei der Katze:24 Vorbeugung von Problemen in der Katzenhaltung, erschienen in Verhaltensmedizin bei Hund und Katze, 2016

Untersuchungen zur Zeckenfauna bei Katzen in Niederbayern, von Nitschke, Katja, 12.07.2014

Akute Schmerzen bei Katzen erkennen – Ein Leitfaden für die Praxis, von Robertson, Sheilah A erschienen in Kleintier konkret, 01.12.2010

Stressbestimmung bei Katzen mit Flohbefall, von Greiner, Lena, 09.02.2013

Das Hobbythek-Katzenbuch: Tips und Rezepte für gesundes Futter und natürliche Pflege, 1. Aufl., von Norten, Ellen Pütz, Jean, 1997

Cattitude: Wie wir Katzen in der Tierarztpraxis verstehen und ihnen das Leben leichter machen. Zusatzmaterial online: Protokolle und Besitzerfragebögen, von Drensler, Angelika, 2018

Empfehlung zur Bekämpfung von Würmern bei Hunden und Katzen, von Schnieder, Thomas erschienen in team spiegel, 01.02.2008

Gesunde Katzen: Schmusen ohne Gefahr, von Mehlhorn, Birgit Mehlhorn, Heinz, 1993

Wenn Katzen älter werden: Gesund und fit bis ins hohe Alter, von Vorbrich, Susanne, 2015

Wenn Katzen kochen könnten: Leckeres für Naschkatzen und Gourmets, von Cramer, Traute, 2015

Katzen: Verhalten . Pflege und Haltung . Rassen, von Claire Bessant, 2008

Die grosse Enzyklopädie der Katzen: Rassen - Haltung – Pflege, von Paddy Cutts, 2006

Alles über Katzen: Haltung, Pflege, Rassen, von Gerber, Bärbel Bielfeld, Horst, 1983

Sphynx: Die nackte Wahrheit (Welt der Katzen), Marcus Skupin, 2017

IMPRINT

1st Edition

 Publisher: Martin Seidel und Corinna Krupp, Bachstraße 37, 53498 Bad Breisig, email: info@expertengruppeverlag.de, Cover photo: www.depositphotos.com. All content in this book is exclusively presented as neutral information. It does not intend to recommend or advertise any of the methods described or mentioned therein. This book does not claim to be complete, nor can the topicality or accuracy of the information offered be guaranteed. This work is not intended to replace expert advice or care from a veterinary surgeon or animal psychologist. The author and the publisher are not liable for any inconvenience or damages resulting from use of this book.

Printed in Great Britain
by Amazon

45650731R00106